THE
HONG KONGER
ANTHOLOGY

WRITTEN AND ILLUSTRATED BY

SOPHIA HOTUNG

The Kylin Archive

The Kylin Archive

First published in Hong Kong in 2021 by
Sophia Hotung

This edition published December 2021

Copyright © 2021 by Sophia Hotung
Illustrations by Sophia Hotung
Translations by Sean Ngiam

All rights reserved. No part of this publication may be reproduced, stored in a retrieval system, or transmitted by any means, without the prior permission in writing of the publisher, nor be otherwise circulated in any form of binding or cover other than that in which it is published and without a similar condition including this condition being imposed on the subsequent purchaser.

ISBN: 979-875-94845-3-0

Book design by Sophia Hotung

Printed and bound by Kindle Direct Publishing

www.sophiahotung.com

THE
HONG KONGER
ANTHOLOGY

WRITTEN AND ILLUSTRATED BY

SOPHIA HOTUNG

The Kylin Archive

For Amy Poon Mills,
my Popo

CONTENTS

Colonia Babylonia 9

Shelf Reflection 11

Hike Don't Hunt 13

High Junk Reef 15

Hog Walker 17

Ghosts of Punters Past 19

Crossing Over 21

Water Break 23

Welcome Party 25

Day Off 27

Bamboo Builders 29

Dimsum Dénouement 31

High Dive 33

Campbell's Troupe 35

Role Models 37

Potential 39

Half the Sky 41

CONTENTS

Tiger Mom Tattoos ... 43

Fountain of Youth ... 45

Ding Dong ... 47

Choi Hung ... 49

Cable Guys ... 51

Bubble Teens ... 53

Time Difference ... 55

[Redacted] ... 57

Hot Girl Bummer ... 59

LKF ... 61

Cupidity ... 63

Happy Hour ... 65

Extra Extra ... 67

Lion Rock Station ... 69

Bao Bei's Feast ... 71

Pharmacist ... 73

Baps & Baos ... 75

CONTENTS

Penthouse	79
After Hours	81
10,000 Faeries	83
Weekday Warriors	85
Room with a View	87
Peak Trail	89
Pigs in Blankets	91
Hong Kong Moms	93
Horoscope Zoetrope	95
View of the World from M&S	97
Dark Side	99
Dragon Riders	101
Yacht Yahoos	103
Pink Ladies	105
Groundlings	107
Autotoll	109
Closing Time	111

CONTENTS

Kowloon Motor Battalion 115

Scaffolds & Spills 117

Opera Girl 119

Mallseum 121

Splash Harbour 123

Just Cabbied 125

St John's Cathedral 127

Courtship 129

Valentine's Cards 131

Chicken & Duck 133

Tai Tai's Toy Boys 135

New Year Transit 137

Zodiac Divers 139

Mooncake Maven 141

Santa at the Cha Chaan Teng 143

Junk of the Magi 145

Portals 147

HOW TO READ THIS BOOK

Thank you for opening this book. You don't really need to read this page, and if you're reading this in a bookstore at the moment, I strongly encourage you to visit pages 16, 58, or 98 to really see what this ramshackle collection is all about. If you're feeling stubborn, you can keep reading this page. However, in return, I will patronisingly instruct you on how to read this book.

This book has three main components, which will determine how you consume it:

First, there is the art. The prints. What I'm imagining most people are coming to this book for. Pretty pictures of Hong Kong based on the New Yorker magazine covers. If you're a "visual learner", feel free to flip through these pages on your sofa or in a dentist's waiting room, and glance perfunctorily at the various prints. You can always scan the QR codes to compare and contrast them against the New Yorker covers that inspired them. If you don't want to scan QR codes, you can also track down the original New Yorkers by looking up the date on each Hong Konger. I kept the dates the same as their American counterparts. All this will certainly take up at least a good hour if you spend about 51 seconds on each spread. Have fun.

Second, there are the poems. No one wanted me to write poems. My mother told me no one would buy my book of poems. No one reads poems. So, don't worry. I've set my expectations low — you can skip the poems.

Third, there are artist's notes. I am the artist. They are my notes. You can read them if you're curious about hidden messages, meanings, and motifs in the prints and poems (but the latter won't be of interest to you since I've been assured that no one will read the poems). To give you a sense of the Easter eggs I hide in prints, I can tell you an anecdote about the print Courtship. I sold it to a couple who put it on their wall and only learned when I told them a week after that there is a little rainbow on the tarmac that symbolises hope. Now, I can't go around to everyone's house to point out little things like hopeful rainbows, so that's why we have the artist's notes.

THE HONG KONGER ANTHOLOGY

On second thought, I would actually quite like you to read the poems. I spent a long time on (some of) them and I think they're fun. After listening to some herself, my mother even thought some were fun. A few of you will recognise a few of them. That's because, much like how a handful of New Yorker covers inspired my Hong Kongers, a handful of well-known poetry inspired my poems. You'll note that the poems don't have punctuation. That's not so much an e.e. cummings rip-off than it is an attempt to do away with punctuation in the same way that ancient Chinese poetry does. (Also, this style worked really well for Rupi Kaur.)

You may be questioning the order of the prints. There is an order, and the poems and prints are best consumed in the order I have laid them out. I thought about alphabetising, chronologising, randomising, but have opted to create a narrative in which relevant or complementary prints, stories, and poems flow one after the other.

If you've read this far and are still standing in the bookstore wondering whether to buy this book, I highly recommend that you try out a couple of the pages near the middle or end before putting this down and running away. It gets better.

FOREWORD

The Hong Konger started as a joke. Bedridden from autoimmune diseases, I started learning to draw on a freshly unboxed iPad on December 25th, 2020. By early spring, I was posting doodles on Instagram, hankering for pity likes. One doodle I worked on was a Hong Kong version of Saul Steinberg's New Yorker cover, View of the World from 9th Avenue. In my version, the joke would show a Hong Kong expatriate's view of the world from Repulse Bay, and I would replace the masthead with "The Hong Konger".

I never posted that first Hong Konger attempt. It never looked right, and I knew I was on to something that just needed more time incubating in my brain. I had been trying to tap into a zeitgeist and had garnered mild recognition by making posters of 1990s Hong Kong from old childhood photographs, but I was looking for my next "thing". The Hong Kong take on Steinberg felt like something that would capture imaginations more than anything else I had so far conceived. So, I set out to create a series of Hong Kongers. I planned to make 12 for a calendar. Now there are over 70.

Much like many Hong Kongers, I am not what you think of when you think of a Hong Konger. The most noticeable thing about me is how astonishingly white I am for a Eurasian. I come from a long line of Eurasians and am the younger daughter of the oldest son of the oldest son of the oldest son of a man called Robert, who is considered our family's bigwig patriarch (not sure if he used the word "bigwig" himself. Will check.)

Besides being astonishingly white for a Eurasian, I am also astonishingly functional-looking for a disabled person. My great-great aunt, Jean Gittins, wrote in her book Stanley: Behind the Barbed Wire that her father, the aforementioned bigwig Great-great-grandpa Robert, had a "mysterious digestive ailment" that "curtailed his activities" and "forced [him] to lead the rest of his life as a semi-invalid." I don't know what's in our genes, but I have some of that digestion-themed semi-invalidity in me too, which has, since the age of 16, caused me to lead an isolated life of inescapable relapse and forced patience.

THE HONG KONGER ANTHOLOGY

I bring this up, because my Eurasian and disabled identities heavily influence the work in this book. You'll glean an identity crisis of what it means to be a Hong Konger who isn't wholly Chinese or not wholly assimilated, what it means to be disabled when you've been fed the "hard work equals success" narrative, what it means when those things intersect. It sounds niche, but the theme of ostracisation in this book will likely relate to anyone's sense of belonging (or not belonging) and theme of disability in this book will likely relate to anyone's sense of futility. There is nostalgia, kinship, and acceptance in this book. There is a celebration of what Hong Kong is, and it is a celebration of diversity and community.

I am and was acutely aware while creating this anthology that my viewpoint is not representative of all Hong Kongers. This anthology contains the perspective of a privileged, native English-speaking, international school-educated, white-passing, Eurasian, sickly woman. I heavily contemplated representation in this book and questioned whether my voice was allowed to be so prevalent when it is not representative of the standard Hong Kong experience (whatever that is). However, this book was never meant to be a field guide to Hong Kong, to be the ambassador of Hong Kong culture, to be the tome we present to the world to cry, "This is us!"

This is a compendium of drawings and rhymes that I made during a year of depression, loss, and loneliness mourning a body, future, and lifestyle that I believed I had earned. This is a journal of recovery and reinvention, and I believe its messages, though specific to myself, can be extrapolated to others and Hong Kong. Finally, this book is a meditation on returning home to one's stead, one's self, and one's calling.

SOPHIA HOTUNG

POETRY REFERENCES

Certain Hong Kongers are accompanied by poems that have been
adapted from or are inspired by popular western and Chinese poetry

Water Break	*Travelling Early to Shangshan* by Wen Tingjun
Welcome Party	*Visiting the Temple of Auspicious Fortune Alone on Winter Solstice* by Su Shi
Day Off	*Happiness* by Raymond Carver
Dimsum Dénouement	*Piano Man* by Billy Joel
Tiger Mom Tattoos	*The Porter's monologue, Macbeth* by William Shakespeare
Time Difference	*Nostalgia* by Yu Guangzhong and *Jerusalem* by William Blake
Extra Extra	Selected poems by Emily Dickinson
Afternoon Tea	*Seeing Off Meng Haoran for Guangling at Yellow Crane Tower* by Li Bai
Pharmacist	*Ode on Melancholy* and *Ode to a Nightingale* by John Keats
10,000 Faeries	*Diving into the Wreck* by Adrienne Rich
Weekday Warriors	*I Do Not Love You Except Because I Love You* by Pablo Neruda
Pigs in Blankets	*Anahorish 1944* by Seamus Heaney
View of the World from M&S	*On First Looking Into Chapman's Homer* by John Keats
Dark Side	*The Destruction of Sennacherib* by Lord Byron
Dragon Riders	*Deep in Spring, the Rain Has Passed (Picking Mulberries)* by Ouyang Xiu
Yacht Yahoos	*Sun and Rain* by Yue Fu
Closing Time	*Ozymandias* by Percy Bysshe Shelley
Mallseum	*A Name* by Ada Limón
Splash Harbour	*The Love Song of J. Alfred Prufrock* by T.S. Eliot
Chicken & Duck	*Ode to the Goose* by Luo Binwang
Tai Tai's Toy Boys	*My Last Duchess* by Robert Browning
Courtship	Sonnets by John Keats, William Shakespeare, and Ben Jonson
Zodiac Divers	*The Mock Turtle's Song* by Lewis Carroll
Junk of the Magi	*Diving into the Wreck* by Adrienne Rich

THE HONG KONGER ANTHOLOGY

HONG KONGERS ABOUT ANIMALS

Chicken & Duck, High Junk Reef, Hog Walker, Horoscope Zoetrope, New Year Transit, Peak Trail, Pigs in Blankets, Room With a View, Weekday Warriors, Zodiac Divers

HONG KONGERS ABOUT CHILDHOOD

Bao Bei's Feast, Bubble Teens, Cable Guys, Campbell's Troupe, Choi Hung, Ding Dong, Fountain of Youth, Happy Hour, Pigs in Blankets, Potential, [Redacted], Role Models, Tiger Mom Tattoos, Time Difference, Zodiac Divers

HONG KONGERS ABOUT HERITAGE

10,000 Faeries, Baps & Baos, Colonia Babylonia, Horoscope Zoetrope, Junk of the Magi, Order Up, Pharmacist, Pigs in Blankets, Pink Ladies, Portals, Shelf Reflection

HONG KONGERS ABOUT HOLIDAYS

Ding Dong, Dragon Riders, Horoscope Zoetrope, Junk of the Magi, Mooncake Maven, New Year Transit, Santa at the Cha Chaan Teng, Valentine's Cards, Zodiac Divers

HONG KONGERS ABOUT FAMILY

Afternoon Tea, Baps & Baos, Dark Side, Hong Kong Moms, Hot Girl Bummer, Just Cabbied, Penthouse, St John's Cathedral, Tiger Mom Tattoos, Time Difference

HONG KONGERS ABOUT FOOD

Afternoon Tea, Bao Bei's Feast, Baps & Baos, Bubble Teens, Closing Time, Dimsum Dénouement, Mooncake Maven, Order Up, Pigs in Blankets, Room With a View, Santa at the Cha Chaan Teng

HONG KONGERS ABOUT LANDMARKS

10,000 Faeries, After Hours, Cable Guys, Campbell's Troupe, Choi Hung, Colonia Babylonia, Dark Side, Fountain of Youth, Ghosts of Punters Past, Groundlings, High Junk Reef, Hike Don't Hunt, High Dive, Hot Girl Bummer, Lion Rock Station, LKF, Peak Trail, Scaffolds & Spills, Shelf Reflection, Splash Harbour, St John's Cathedral, View of the World from M&S, Water Break, Yacht Yahoos

HONG KONGERS ABOUT LEISURE

After Hours, Autotoll, Cable Guys, Campbell's Troupe, Chicken & Duck, Choi Hung, Dragon Riders, Ghosts of Punters Past, Groundlings, High Dive, LKF, Lion Rock Station, Mallseum, Opera Girl, Peak Trail, Splash Harbour, Valentine's Cards, Yacht Yahoos

HONG KONGERS ABOUT LOVE

Bubble Teens, Courtship, Cupidity, Baps & Baos, Just Cabbied, St John's Cathedral, Tai Tai's Toy Boys, Valentine's Cards

HONG KONGERS ABOUT NIGHTLIFE

After Hours, Closing Time, Ding Dong, Ghosts of Punters Past, Groundlings, Half the Sky, Kowloon Motor Battalion, Just Cabbied, LKF, Mooncake Maven, Santa at the Cha Chaan Teng, Tai Tai's Toy Boys

HONG KONGERS ABOUT POLITICS

Baps & Baos, Colonia Babylonia, Courtship, [Redacted], Time Difference, Welcome Party

HONG KONGERS ABOUT TRANSPORTATION

Autotoll, Cable Guys, Colonia Babylonia, Closing Time, Crossing Over, Dark Side, Dragon Riders, Just Cabbied, Kowloon Motor Battalion, Lion Rock Station, New Year Transit, Role Models, Yacht Yahoos

HONG KONGERS ABOUT WOMEN

Campbell's Troupe, Crossing Over, Cupidity, Day Off, Dimsum Dénouement, Extra Extra, Half the Sky, Happy Hour, High Dive, Hog Walker, Hong Kong Moms, Hot Girl Bummer, Opera Girl, Peak Trail, Penthouse, Pharmacist, Pink Ladies, Potential, [Redacted], Role Models, Tai Tai's Toy Boys, Tiger Mom Tattoos, Water Break

HONG KONGERS ABOUT WORK

After Hours, Bamboo Builders, Baps & Baos, Closing Time, Crossing Over, Day Off, Dimsum Dénouement, Extra Extra, Fountain of Youth, Half the Sky, Happy Hour, Hog Walker, Opera Girl, Order Up, Penthouse, Pharmacist, Pigs in Blankets, Potential, [Redacted], Scaffolds & Spills, Tiger Mom Tattoos, Water Break

THE HONG KONGER ANTHOLOGY

back then the rock had but one tongue 'til vicky came around
down on the delta she found our lot and built herself a town
she baked bricks and churned cement and built a tower block
one so high it graced the sky that sheltered our small rock

let us build a city get the concrete grind the shale
they'll speak of us in leicester square and in maida vale
brick by brick she bridled men she'd dragged in from the fields
and oohed and aahed at charts of bars and lines that showed great yields

who would come to audit and survey the structure's base
the boxers are all doped and brawling up in warlord space
vicky's mates all chortle blumber cockney scouser slang
there's no word in edgewise when the geordies join the gang

stop them all from talking though then have them work confused
throw in canto cussing and blow the safety fuse
confound them with our idioms make them lose their face
then we'll see how vicky fares with termites in the place

set the hardest lessons with twelve tones maybe nine
their deaf ears pitch them poorly all while we hear them just fine
they'll spend all day just squabbling oi oi wots this duh-no
they'll find the block so bad the rock will once again be home

Colonia Babylonia melds the biblical story of the Tower of Babel with real art on matchboxes from colonial-era Hong Kong restaurants, bars, and clubs. Initially, I planned to draw popular Hong Kong brands on the ad spaces, but given the biblical context, I opted to depict establishments from late 20th-century Hong Kong. My Hong Konger mother helped me pinpoint recognisable sixties and seventies establishments from a selection of matchboxes I had found, and I also included some of my childhood favourites that introduced fancy European food to me, like The Peninsula Hotel's Swiss restaurant, Chesa (where I had my first cheese fondue) and Jimmy's Kitchen (where I had my first chicken kiev). The poem is partly a satire that attributes the fall of British reign in Hong Kong to British people's inability to grasp Cantonese and speak the same language as local Hong Kongers, much like the denizens of Babel were unable to communicate when they spoke different languages.

SOPHIA HOTUNG

COLONIA BABYLONIA 巴比 • Hong Kong's own Tower of Babel advertises popular colonial-era bars, restaurants, and clubs. Based on the October 2, 1995 New Yorker magazine cover by Edward Sorel.

THE HONG KONGER ANTHOLOGY

you found yourself in tst waiting to cross the way
your phone had died you could not spy the route post-docked ferry
a wizened crone of plasticked garb red and white and blue
shuffled along through the throng to hand a sheath to you
sepia-toned and frayed on edge an antique shelf of teak
you couldn't ask before she left with naught but her traveller's wreak
boarding you surveyed the shelf depicted in your hand
a book some beans a flask some balm of seahorse corpses canned
a mounted trout a porcine bank an abacus for play
a plushy seal a stash of gin a bauhinia and skates
the relics of an equine race a beer-soaked rugby ball
a glass of water binocs cap dance shoes camping haul
bottled ships her majesty's fleet a beach ball wedged beneath
a pail spade morbid enclave a carabiner's wreath
you stomach the waves that lap lick languish through the tide
when you look up your breath does stop to see the island side

Shelf Reflection's New Yorker counterpart shows a Manhattan-shaped bookcase with different decorations signifying the geography of the island: a houseplant for Central Park, skates for Madison Square Garden, and a graduation cap for New York University. I liked the idea of breaking Hong Kong Island down into its neighbourhoods with equivalent symbols. From top to bottom, you'll see books for Hong Kong University; cafetieres for gentrified coffee shops in Kennedy Town; Chinese medicine for Sai Ying Pun; a mounted fish for Aberdeen; an abacus and piggy bank for Central; alcohol for Wan Chai; a plushie sea lion toy for Ocean Park; horse racing paraphernalia for Happy Valley; a bauhinia for Golden Bauhinia Square; binoculars and a cap for hiking Jardine's Lookout; rugby and beer for the Rugby Sevens at Hong Kong Stadium; a glass of water for the Tai Tam Reservoirs; a ship for Stanley and Repulse Bay; hiking equipment for Tai Tam Country Park; ice skates for Cityplaza's ice rink; ballet slippers for Youth Square in Chai Wan; a skull and cemetery snow globe for Sai Wan War Cemetery, Chai Wan Muslim Cemetery, Holy Cross Catholic Cemetery, and Hong Kong Buddhist Cemetery; a beach ball, spade, and bucket for Shek O Beach; and camping gear for Shek O Country Park. If you're still not seeing the shape of Hong Kong Island at all, turn the book 90° to the left.

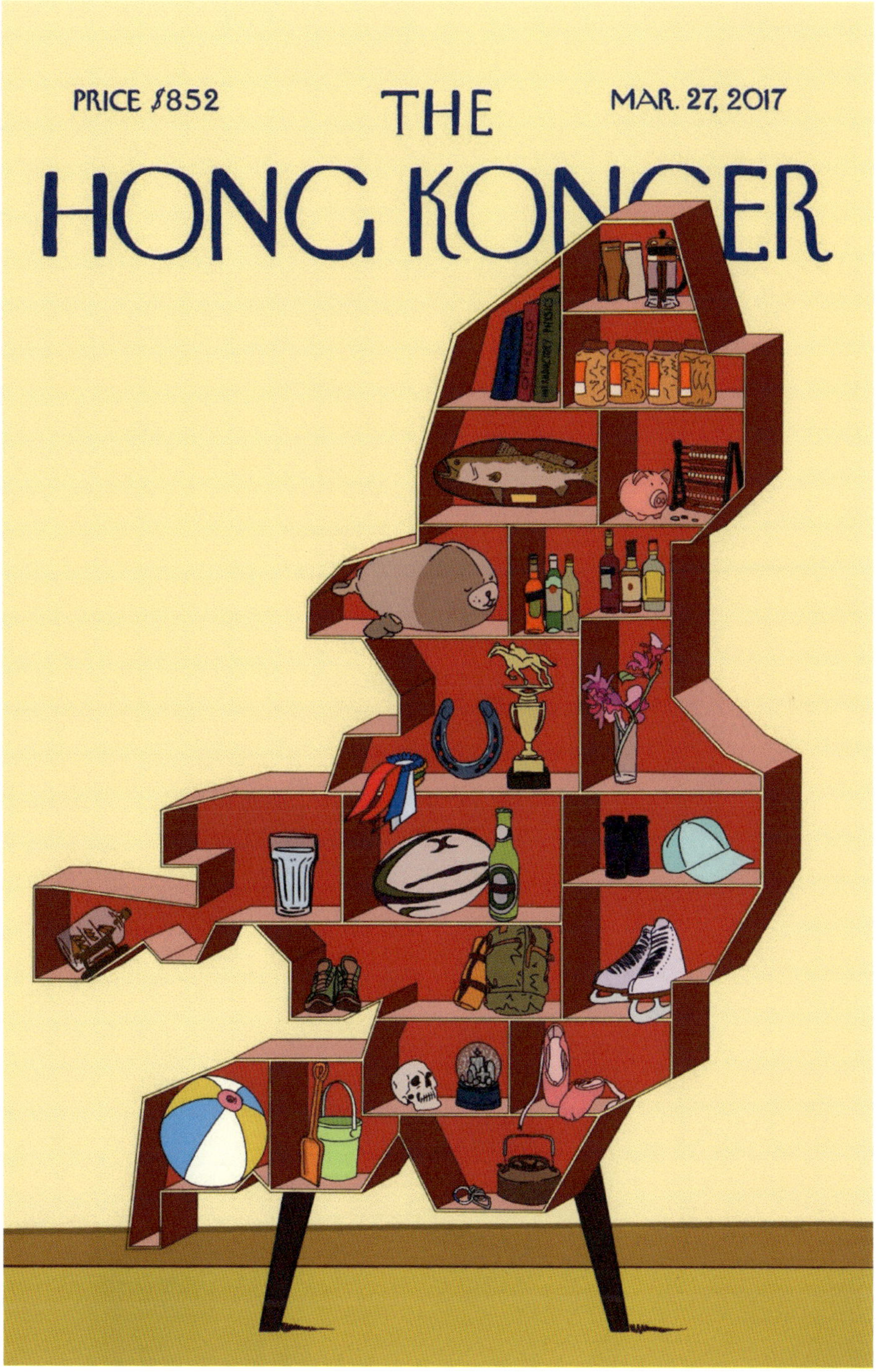

SOPHIA HOTUNG

SHELF REFLECTION 鰂魚條紋 • A Hong Kong Island-shaped bookcase holds knick-knacks that represent various landmarks. Based on the March 27, 2017 New Yorker magazine cover *Shelf Life* by Luci Gutiérrez.

11

what do you do with an island
that cannot feed itself
how are the birds and the snakes
not husks parched and drying
why do we not find carcasses
lying in the way
or have monkeys hobble up to us
crusted and craving palms cupped
for a drip from our flasks
we had to build these monuments
and catch the rain in our hands
the will of men knows no decorum
this dry rock be dammed

Hike Don't Hunt began as a comment on hunting. The original New Yorker cover depicts hunters foraying into the forest. I thought it was interesting that New Yorkers venture into woods to hunt while Hong Kongers venture into country parks to hike. I prefer the Hong Kong pastime personally. Musings while making the print changed as I thought more about Hong Kong's history of water filtration and purification (thrilling, I know). The beginning of James Clavell's novel *Tai Pan* begins with the protagonist arriving in Hong Kong in 1842, at a point during which the island was just a dry rock. An argument ensues between the characters about whether the rock is even habitable given the lack of potable water. In real life, to combat Hong Kong's inherent aridness, the British commissioned the construction of reservoirs to collect rainwater. Now, 70 to 80% of our water is imported from Dongjiang, but prior to the 21st century, water rationing was common among Hong Kongers, who relied heavily on reservoirs like Tai Tam's.

SOPHIA HOTUNG

HIKE DON'T HUNT 逃水行舟 • Hikers trek along the narrow winding roads along the Tai Tam Tuk Reservoir Masonry Bridge. Based on the October 18, 1941 New Yorker magazine cover by Roger Duvoisin.

THE HONG KONGER ANTHOLOGY

> this picture would be so much nicer
> if you didn't include those bags
> that's the point of the picture i said
> as we slurped shark fin soup

High Junk Reef depicts High Junk Peak not only because that mountain is one of the sharpest peaks in Hong Kong and therefore makes for a picturesque silhouette, but also because of the pun on "junk". (I love me a pun.) I wanted to depict sea life all native to Hong Kong, and make them almost unrealistically vibrant, detailed, and beautiful. Once I did that, however, I trapped them in plastic bags and definned an unsuspecting shark. I'll be the first to say that this is not a subtle take on maritime conservation, but my goal was to make something beautiful, then ruin it with rubbish and violence as a tribute to real life.

SOPHIA HOTUNG

HIGH JUNK REEF 膠袋加玉鼉鳴 • Hong Kong sea creatures go about their daily business, encumbered by environmental destruction. Based on the January 20, 1968 New Yorker cover *Under the Sea* by Charles Samuel Addams.

15

THE HONG KONGER ANTHOLOGY

it seemed the perfect summer job to dally in the sun
to collect fees and tie up shoes and hit up the dog run
ms ma paid me three hundred to leash up her mutt drake
and jayden wong paid five hundred to care for his pet snake
twinkle cheung paid extra from her day job's till
to get special treatment for her elderly spoonbill
jerome lent me his gecko kyle lent his sow
and farmer gong from north sai kung gave his brooding cow
rainbow lent her monkey and aaron kwan his bat
mason lent his pangolin tortoise and civet cat
the grasshopper and mongoose were both from caroline
and mr snode from borrett road lent his porcupine
so we all walked together a parade of merry beasts
all could heel and no one squealed at the rigid leash
we then came to the dog run and so as not to smother
i unhooked all the leads to find that they'd all eat each other

Hog Walker depicts animals that, like the sea life in *High Junk Reef*, are all native to Hong Kong's back and beyond. Originally, the setting was a non-descript beach, but I found that the beach did not shout "This is in Hong Kong!" as loudly as a Wan Chai landmark like the Star Street Refuse Collection Point. I also noticed that when I used a beach as a background, the gecko (currently latched onto a wall) ended up floating in mid-air... a slight artistic oversight. A few people have asked me if *Hog Walker*, like *High Junk Reef*, is a comment on conservation with the refuse centre representing the polluting of habitats, but really, it isn't. I just wanted to incorporate the Mondrian-style wall of the building.

SOPHIA HOTUNG

HOG WALKER 萬獸山秀 • A woman walks a leash-load of Hong Kong wildlife past the Star Street Refuse Collection Point. Based on the June 21, 2021 New Yorker magazine cover *Local Fauna* by Peter de Sève.

they come to watch the races once their betters go to bed
but on these nights the steeds canter anti-clock instead
aethon leads the way much to the cheers of old man gong
and branded by the gods of hell alastor comes second
these phantoms of the valley's plague all died in choke and doubt
so let them punt their obuli on a nice night out

Ghosts of Punters Past's New Yorker counterpart shows the Aqueduct Racetrack in Queens with people betting on the sidelines. When I first saw the New Yorker cover, I thought the people were ghosts. The combination of racecourse plus ghosts immediately conjured ideas of St Michael's Cemetery across the road from the Happy Valley Racecourse. It made me want to depict ghosts watching the races. One thing to note is that the horses go around clockwise in Hong Kong and anti-clockwise in New York. I've seamlessly logicked my way out of that in the poem by implying that, because we're in some alternative underworld, everything goes backwards, as if time has reversed to raise the dead for Wednesday race night. I remember when I was a kid visiting the cemetery to see my ancestors' graves. It always looked like such a haunted, fairytale place despite being next to a flyover and tunnel. The history also fascinates about how the British military men who set up camp in Happy Valley contracted malaria in 1840 because of poor sewer drainage. There were so many bodies that they just had to bury them where they were and make a cemetery. The poem references Old Man Gong, whose name may ring a bell if you're reading this book chronologically. *Hog Walker* mentions Farmer Gong (flip back a page if you need a memory refresher), who I have decided is a descendant of the phantom punter.

SOPHIA HOTUNG

GHOSTS OF PUNTERS PAST 今夕吾驅歸馬場 • Ghosts come down from Hong Kong Cemetery to watch the racing at Happy Valley Racecourse. Based on the May 12, 1962 New Yorker magazine cover by Garrett Price.

keep the sun off your back and off of your face
off the fish in the market stall
you'll take the governor up the trail
when the men wear out their soles

bid farewell through a fence to the man you loved
he is skinny now beaten and frayed
then ration out juk in the prison cell room
catching salt breeze chokes from the bay

learn shorthand squiggles sit tight at your desk
do not stand or they'll pinch you and grin
bound feet now seem sweet to the stiff kitten heels
they insist that you strut in

spawn a sprog deck them out bno
so their passport's their safety net
then wrap them in masks and spray them with gel
and hide them from all they have met

send them off to school to read books they don't like
then join the march through wan chai
greet tanks rolling through not that they used to
and bid the motherland hi

Crossing Over's date-labelled panels signify different years for female workers in Hong Kong. The 1912 panel shows standard dawn-of-the-century garb that both female and male outdoor workers would have worn. In 1926, most rickshaw drivers were men but, on occasion, women would drive when male family members were injured, resting, or retired. The 1942 panel is a tribute to my great-great aunt, Jean Gittins, who served as a hospital administrator at Hong Kong University and was interned at Stanley by the Japanese during the Second World War. She last saw her husband through a fence of another prison camp in Kowloon, which I referenced in the second stanza of the poem. The 1968 panel is also a tribute, this one to my maternal grandma or Popo who worked in the Hong Kong government during the 1950s and 60s. She won a scholarship to an American university as a teenager but was barred from going on account of being a woman. Throughout her life, she battled institutional racialised misogyny ranging from strangers thinking she was her Eurasian daughters' amah not mother, to watching her male colleagues receive housing benefits to which she was not entitled. The subject is holding a Hong Kong BNO passport to represent the 1997 handover and Hong Kongers who migrated to the United Kingdom for new opportunities. 2003 shows the SARS epidemic and is a tribute to my own mother who kept her business running at a time when she had no way of seeing to customers. 2014 and 2019 represent the pro-democracy protests, while 2047 represents the end of Hong Kong's status as a special administrative region and its full return to China.

CROSSING OVER 玉女寧後 • Women workers from various years of Hong Kong's past and future cross Des Voeux Road. Based on the November 24, 2014 New Yorker magazine cover *Time Warp* by Richard McGuire.

THE HONG KONGER ANTHOLOGY

in the morning she starts to move pre-alarm
travelling thinking numbly of home
a tram dings an overturned bin
the moon still up on the edge of the mount
footsteps warming the dew
leaves fell from hiking trails overnight
bougainvillea bloomed and wilted
a straw ended broom undefined stickiness
on its handle
to sweep and sweat sweep and sweat
nature's groundkeeper

Water Break's poem is an adaptation of Wen Tingjun's poem *Travelling Early to Shangshan*, which begins: "In the morning, he starts to move at the journey bell". Wen's is a poem that conjures a sense of undisturbed nature. In *Water Break*'s poem, I wanted to convey the idea that, through its indifference to human activity, nature makes a mess, sheds its leaves, and rains down on people regardless of just desserts. A similar concept is explored in my Hong Konger, *Dragon Riders*. I created *Water Break* as a tribute to Hong Kong's sanitation workers, with the 2019 protests and subsequent street clean-ups in mind. The idea of nature being unsympathetic to labour, even causing more work through natural decay, was something I wanted to explore.

WATER BREAK 起 • A sanitation worker takes a water break on Oil Street. Based on the April 20, 2020 New Yorker magazine cover *After the Shift* by Owen Smith.

the man at the desk with his heavy cludding stamps
is not impressed with the leaves in my hair
he is wrinkling his nose at the stench of the swamp
we waded through between here and the gate

but i put on a smile and run my dry tongue
along the backs of my teeth scanning for morsels
of food i ate when they sent me off
for greener pastures and greener bills

he looks down at my papers and up at my eyes
and a moment stands where i hope he will warm
but he exhales the stench of the crocodile piss
and slams my book shut with a thump

the well has no warmth the rain has drowned roots
there's no space for flowers and i've come alone

Welcome Party's equivalent New Yorker shows three lines at airport immigration: one for U.S. citizens, one for non-citizens, and one for Eurotrash. Racial inequality in Hong Kong manifests as tacit segregation by way of gentrification; prejudice by employers, landlords, and service workers; and even different immigration rules depending on nationality. For instance, a banker may live in Hong Kong as an expatriate, and after seven years can receive permanent resident status. Meanwhile, an individual on a domestic worker visa would never receive permanent resident status, even after working in Hong Kong for over 40 years. For gweilos and white-passing Hong Kongers like myself, authority figures will often shoo us away rather than properly penalise us, service can often be better based on an assumption that white people will spend more generously, and fair complexions are idolised with skin-whitening products. This print was a study on all these issues through satire. The poem draws on Su Shi's *Visiting the Temple of Auspicious Fortune Alone on Winter Solstice*, which jumped out at me as a suitable basis for *Welcome Party*'s poem because of its final line that translates from Chinese to English into: "I find I've come alone."

SOPHIA HOTUNG

WELCOME PARTY 歡迎 • Arrivals into Chek Lap Kok Airport pass through immigration. Based on the October 14 & 21, 2002 New Yorker magazine cover *International Arrivals* by Bruce McCall.

o early it's still almost dark out
i'm at the bus stop parched
and the usual sunday morning texts
are passing through the ether

when i see the girl and her dog
walking down from a trail
panting and no less en route
to a barbecue or junk trip
or back to bed

she wears shoes my daughter talks about
and air pods hang from her ears
those could get lost in a credenza at home
and no one would ever know

it's early in the morning
and families drive around together
they zhoom by slowly my bus is late
the sky is taking on light
though the moon still hangs over the harbour
such beauty that for a minute

longing and loneliness
loss and love
don't enter into this
happiness

it comes on then goes
comes on and goes beyond
any sunday morning talk about it

Day Off was a print I knew I had to create to round out the collection and represent overseas domestic workers, but it took a while to identify the perfect New Yorker cover to adapt. I researched New Yorker covers using keywords like "mother", "household", even "maid" to capture a sense of foreign domestic workers' labour and living situations, but none seemed right until I happened upon Alajalov's illustration of World War II munitions workers on a lunch break. The pods of workers on a break brought to mind the pods of domestic workers on a Sunday, and thus *Day Off* was born. I used bright colours and added playful details like the Jollibee chicken bucket and nail polish to contrast against the underlying struggles of foreign domestic workers in Hong Kong. When penning the poem, I opted to mirror Raymond Carver's *Happiness*, because I felt overwhelmed by the volume of issues I could discuss and wanted a laconic poet to convey the insurmountable burden tersely.

DAY OFF 吃得是福 • Domestic workers eat lunch on the Circular Pedestrian Bridge in Causeway Bay during their day off. Based on the September 5, 1942 New Yorker magazine cover by Constantin Alajalov.

do not worry
i will get an egg mayonnaise sandwich
from the corner before i reach the station
if i've time to spare i'll down
a paper cup of tea there too
i'm bound to finish one triangle while waiting
for the conductor to bring along my poles
i will wrap my leftover egg and bread
and wedge it between drill and screw
my laces i'll fasten to the stilt tips
knot-tight the way i teach the boys
and tread my way o'er ground and sea
to wherever the cranes have called me to
and should i misstep or slip or fall
i do not need your grief and rage
for whom else will balance on panda food
to erect the monuments of our age

Bamboo Builders' New Yorker equivalent features businessmen commuting precariously on stilts. Pairing a mundane commute with a bizarre mode of transport inspired me to craft an equally incongruous poem. The ensuing poem captured the routine nature of a commute, a 7-11 on-the-go breakfast, idle chat with the wife about the kids, and a paper cup of tea, but then married it with a zany world where, instead of catching a train, some sort of conductor provides commuters with bamboo scaffolding to lace onto their feet to get to work. I wanted to include an element of stoicism and anxiety over the dangerous nature of construction work by fusing a humdrum morning routine and silly phrases like "panda food" with the morbid risks of balancing on wood, storeys and storeys above the ground.

SOPHIA HOTUNG

BAMBOO BUILDERS 視險若夷 • Construction workers traverse Hong Kong on bamboo scaffolding stilts. Based on the September 12, 1994 New Yorker magazine cover by Eric Drooker.

THE HONG KONGER ANTHOLOGY

it's 3pm on a saturday
the regular crowd's shuffled out
ah tse is piling up teapots
careful not to spill dregs from the spout

she screams ah wong stop eating that hargau
and those leftover chasiubaos
i'm sure that those dantat from tuesday
got lost when they fell in your mouth

liu jeh runs a promising foodstagram
tsang mui has a boyfriend who's white
but you can be betting you'll still find them sweating
over smoothing out tablecloths right

and that waitress is folding napkin cranes
and she's fetching strong bleach detergent
to wipe off the seats wet veg and cold meats
in the restaurant's dimsum dénouement

Dimsum Dénouement's poem parodies Billy Joel's *Piano Man*, which begins: "It's nine o'clock on a Saturday, / The regular crowd shuffles in." My maternal grandparents, Popo and Grandpa Lawrie, celebrated their wedding lunch at Maxim's Palace in City Hall and Billy Joel is a favourite car crooner in the family. The print shows vignettes of laborious and/or lazy servers clearing up after a busy lunch hour. The poem reflects the servers' different personalities and predicaments in turn. Originally, I wanted to adapt some of Ludwig Bemelman's rhymes from his *Madeline* books. I used to love *Madeline* and even have a doll of her with her appendix scar, but I let *Madeline* go when crafting the poem because I thought it would be more fun to incorporate a song into the anthology, and *Piano Man* was a symbolic and fitting song that illustrates the different characters' vignettes and explores the theme of labour.

SOPHIA HOTUNG

DIMSUM DENOUEMENT 殘山剩水 • Servers clear tables after lunch at Maxim's Palace in City Hall. Based on the January 3, 1953 New Yorker magazine cover by Ludwig Bemelmans.

THE HONG KONGER ANTHOLOGY

        jump jump cry the swimmers
      on the sidelines of the deep end
         she appears poised and lithe
        a fine match for the boys' team

      she wobbled not once while climbing
      rung by rung to the astroturf board
her pink tongue teasing the jeerers beneath
     vertigo valiant she steps to the edge

       she tucks and pikes and spins twofold
       her movements curl and sweep the air
   weightless for a moment before she catches
          a breath too sharp for ospreys

      to clock when form reformats to fall
      when flight becomes folly and fails
that business of nuance no youngling can spy
  'til she crashes and breaks on her back

High Dive was a print that I wanted to create because its New Yorker equivalent is one of the more iconic covers from the magazine. When thinking about the Hong Konger adaptation, my mind, not surprisingly, went to diving boards. When I was about nine, I went swimming with some friends in the Ladies' Recreation Club's pool, where there are three diving boards one, three, and five metres off the ground (or water, I suppose). We saw an older girl dive off the top board and, being naïve, I asserted that I could do that too. I could not. I rolled forward mid-air and smacked my back so forcefully on the water's surface that I thought I had broken it. The small gathering of children that I had boasted to all watched while I tried to laugh it off. The poem is a retelling of my graceful drop and is based on the 600 BCE poem *The Crying Ospreys*, which is part of an ancient lyric collection known as the *Book of Songs*.

SOPHIA HOTUNG

HIGH DIVE 龍跳虎臥 • A swimmer prepares to launch off the diving board at the Ladies' Recreation Club. Based on the June 19 & 26, 2000 New Yorker magazine cover *Poised* by R. Kenton Nelson.

i've signed you up to learn to dance
to point and flex and leap
wear this swimsuit that's not waterproof
and shoes that don't go on roads
pull your hair so far back
that it nearly falls out your scalp
then every spring play a bush or tree
in the recital i'll come to nine times
the mistress will chide you harshly
keeping time on a tambourine
she'll be the only woman
you'll know who says what she thinks
hate her all you want
and cry while your feet bleed
but conjure her in your woman age
when you don't get what you need

Campbell's Troupe was a piece I planned on scrapping, because it didn't end up looking much like its New Yorker counterpart. However, it resonated so much with me and other Hong Kongers who grew up taking ballet lessons at The Carol Bateman School of Dancing in the basement of The Helena May that I kept it. I used to hate ballet classes and would beg not to go. I finally liberated myself aged nine when I convinced my mother that I would be a better guitarist than ballerina. I can't quite pinpoint why I hated ballet so much. For a long time, I never wanted to be considered graceful, beautiful, or pretty, because, even as a child, I had clocked that there was something about femininity that opened women up to unsolicited comments, unwanted attention, and unnecessary sexualisation. I could not articulate it, but I knew that women were talked over, exploited, fetishised, and disenfranchised more than men. My solution was therefore to avoid all things feminine and try to be one of the boys; this meant no skirts, no tutus, and *no ballet*. When I was thinking of the poem for *Campbell's Troupe*, I wasn't quite sure what to write about. I could write about all my gender angst. I could write about the history of The Helena May as a sanctuary for women who were barred from The Hong Kong Club, but in the end, I wanted to focus on Joan Campbell, the ballet mistress who trained my mum, my sister, and me at The Helena May. She intimidated us all as a ballet mistress because she demanded poise, discipline, and perfection. I remember finding her scary, but then, when I'd see her in The Helena May dining room or around town, she was a lovely, gracious person. It turned out she scared me because she was the only woman I knew who demanded that people meet her expectations. Most other women I knew were accommodating or did what they could to avoid being called "difficult". Not Mrs Campbell. She held us to her high standards and didn't care if we feared her. She is the role model I didn't realise I had. She's an example not because she taught us all how to be ladies with pointed toes and good posture, but because she showed us how to reject anything less than what was demanded.

CAMPBELL'S TROUPE 金寶幫 • Students from the Carol Bateman School of Dancing leave ballet mistress Joan Campbell's ballet class in the basement of The Helena May and ascend Garden Road. Based on the September 29, 1934 New Yorker cover *Housekeepers Cleaning Brownstone House* by Arnold Hall.

THE HONG KONGER ANTHOLOGY

       they sort us into cliques based on eyelash length and bone structure
       and funnel us in two straight lines led by judgement and shame

          pied pipers of the beauty aisle we're led into a cave
          where they speak to us of alter egos lithe shiny gloss

       some girls get word à la pigeons and crackle over radio
         we hear the foe is sweet and less the beast we know
     but who are we if they are what we lack and what we have

            we call them to appear in mirrors
          but these mermaids they don't arrive
        we purge ourselves and set the tinderbox to thighs

     they taunt us through their banners and placards in the street
           tum tight frizz free glitter glow softness
      and us in polyester wool blind to spotting ourselves

Role Models is one of my favourite prints, because everyone reads into it differently. Some people think that I'm taking a stab at conservatively dressed girls, others think I'm shaming lingerie models. My intention was actually to celebrate both ends of the spectrum. All four schoolgirls don't look at the models with disdain but with curiosity and open-mindedness. They also each have the same skin tone and hair colour as the model in front of them. The only person who seems uncomfortable is the teacher, who represents authority and the internalised sexism within women who critique other women for arbitrary attributes. With *Role Models*, I wanted to highlight innocence, beauty, freedom, unity, celebration, and acceptance. Also, because people have asked, any similarity to actual persons, schools, or uniforms, living or dead, is purely coincidental.

ROLE MODELS 醋海生波 • Schoolgirls stare at a billboard of underwear models while walking through Mong Kok MTR Station with their teacher. Based on the May 9, 1959 New Yorker magazine cover by Perry Barlow.

THE HONG KONGER ANTHOLOGY

tonight i lie in bed
another hour left unchanged
yet tomorrow brings helios
and bytes of notes in boxes
i cannot know nor can i fathom
what i will be what i will become
all i know is the stillness of the night
and the boldness of youth
and the pure white unknowing

Potential was inspired by the Hong Kong-based Filipina stand-up comic and jack-of-all-trades Francesca Ayala, whom I interviewed for the book. Ayala, who has worked in journalism, food and beverage, and education — has seen it all: learning centre employers asking her to tell parents that she's Mexican not Filipina, private tutoring parents forbidding her from speaking Tagalog to domestic helpers, or just getting solicited for sex when walking through Wan Chai. This measly footnote won't do her story justice, but our discussion of the intersectional identities of working Filipina women in Hong Kong greatly shaped this print and the Hong Konger project outside of this anthology. The New Yorker equivalent of *Potential* shows a girl thinking about all the ways she might serve her country during World War II, but the Hong Konger depicts a girl with bridled potential. I actually wrote the corresponding poem in March 2014 on my phone just before falling asleep the night prior to hearing back from the Barnard College admissions office. The daunting awareness that my whole future would depend on an email on a tiny screen kept me in this numb void of ignorance that would only dissipate when the schedule admissions emails went out at 6am. The void, which I described as "pure white unknowing", takes on a more sinister meaning in the racialised context of *Potential*, but still conveys the arbitrariness of fate.

SOPHIA HOTUNG

POTENTIAL 前途無限 • A Filipina girl sits alone pondering potential careers from which prejudice and stigma may bar her. Based on the February 27, 1943 New Yorker magazine cover by Constantin Alajalov.

the towers here are one hundred floors high
and when i ride to the top i can scoop up stars
run my hands through their dust as i would through my hair
and feel their soft glitter silken in my palms

i do not dare to run to show you how it feels
to disturb the landlords and men in tails
who sip brandy and cognac unimpressed by the scene
unburdened by the downward rush

a sign by the lift reads in bold serif caps
open roof six to nine glass ceiling removed
we jitter and jostle photograph with our eyes
to recall later the smell of the view

then the hour strikes and our group is ushered
back into the lift so the next tour can see
the fleeting glimpse of a world sold to us
but held overhead like a toy out of reach

the ground floor lobby swarms with sweat
of plebs and prolets and polts
don't be the crowd don't be the throng
appraise then avoid their faults

take it take it don't you want a go
it's yours for the having if you try
we jump and we hop with our hands in the air
brawling to hold up the sky

Half the Sky and *Potential*'s prints and poems complement and contrast each other. *Half the Sky*'s print shows affluent, local women as established fixtures in Hong Kong society and powerful titans of industry, while *Potential* shows an immigrant girl dreaming of hypothetical futures. The poems were also written when I was 19, then 27, and the difference in their tone highlights lessons learnt from coming of age. *Potential*'s poem is naïve and hopeful for a future of success and fulfilment, whereas *Half the Sky*'s poem comes from a cynical perspective of how far women are able or permitted to go in male-dominated spheres. *Half the Sky*'s poem recounts a fictional field trip to a penthouse skyscraper arena of hot-shots that seems only accessible through strategic schmoozing, playing long with the boys' club, and out-competing other women. The print did not start out so cynically. It was created specially for an exhibition to raise funds for gynaecological cancer support. The exhibition's theme was female empowerment, which I conveyed by having women carry Hong Kong's major buildings, and thereby major businesses and economies, on their heads. I did, however, want to draw attention to the exclusivity and classism of the notion that women can make it regardless of ticking racial, behavioural, physical, and cultural boxes, so I made the women curvier than their New Yorker equivalents, and I penned the poem to highlight the persistence of gender inequality in corporate spaces.

SOPHIA HOTUNG

HALF THE SKY 半邊天 • Business tycoons, modelling the International Finance Centre, Lippo Centre, Central Plaza, the Peak Tower, and the Bank of China as hats, assemble among Hong Kong's skyscrapers. Based on the November 8, 1999 New Yorker magazine cover *High Fashion* by Danuta Dabrowska-Siemaszkiewicz.

there's a knocking indeed if a man were porter of gonville
he should have old turning the caius

buzz buzz buzz
here's a mother that hanged her son
on the expectation of clout
come in sit down have a tissue
to wipe his snivelling snout

buzz buzz buzz
here's another that could with no bother
swear at both me and her ward
accuse me of treason with poppycock reason
i cost her a place at Harvard

buzz buzz buzz
here's a tai tai who set up accounts
to send off extortionate fees
to a man with a beard who's at this hour
sitting her son's sats

buzz never at quiet with the drill
of my needle ink quagmire
so i charge large bitcoin bullion
to stoke the everlasting bonfire

Tiger Mom Tattoos is the print my mother calls "the creepy one". I think every parent in Hong Kong struggles to find a balance between pushing their child to meet their full potential and cutting them some slack to let kids be kids. *Tiger Mom Tattoos* takes a stab at parents who figuratively brand their children by instilling in them ideas that their innate worth is the prestigious university that they eventually attend. While the New Yorker cover shows a mother tattooing "Mom" on her son's chest, the Hong Konger shows tattoos of Ivy League crests. The mother has a Yale tattoo, the son is getting a Harvard tattoo, and the tattooist has a Columbia lion, panhellenic lettering, the Bitcoin logo, and even Elon Musk. In the background are pictures of success stories to lure parents inside, almost advertising a self-fulfilling prophecy. My parents were not ever *that* pushy, but I have seen pictures of four-year-old me in a shirt that read, "Yale Class of 20??" and I do remember my mum getting antsy when I was "only" waitlisted for an Ivy, so there's definitely something in the water in Hong Kong. The corresponding poem is adapted from William Shakespeare's Porter's monologue from Act 2, Scene 3 of *Macbeth*. The first line of the monologue begins: "Here's a knocking indeed! If a / man were porter of hell-gate, he should have / old turning the key." I changed it to a pun on the Cambridge University college Gonville & Caius (pronounced "keys"). The Porter is one of those Shakespearean characters that pops up briefly but is researched to death for his significance in the wider play. I can't unleash centuries of Porter conspiracy theories on you here, but in the Hong Konger version of the Porter's monologue, the tattoo artist is speaking and recounting his experiences with various over-zealous tiger parents and their children.

TIGER MOM TATTOOS 刻骨銘心 • A Yale graduate watches a tattoo artist brand her son with the Harvard crest. Based on the May 10, 1993 New Yorker magazine cover *Mother Tattoo* by Art Spiegelman.

what would i be if i had not spent
those nascent years believing
that all i was good for was paper and red ink
shiny stickers and the first few letters of the alphabet
in my wildest dreams of what
freedom and laughter is
all i can picture is a bolobao after kumon
a hot chocolate after the recital
to splash and play in a fountain
only if it taught me to swim
or won me a woven badge on my scout's sash
i am a knot of need for a smile
a kindly glance a smatter of applause
i am what my linkedin says
i am what my report cards wrote home
i am then and then i am not
and then what am i if i am not
a dilly-dallier in cold chlorine

Fountain of Youth is another print inspired by my Popo. My mother used to run one of her Kids' Gallery art schools on Macdonnell Road and my Popo, her mother, lived on Arbuthnot Road. The Hong Kong Botanical and Zoological Gardens therefore was a thoroughfare to get from the former to the latter and back when we were kids. My Popo showed us the flamingos, took us to the playground, and took photos of us posing by the dandelion-like fountain spokes. When I returned to Hong Kong as a 24-year-old, I saw that the fountain had been renovated into a grey, brutalist structure. Given that my Popo had passed away while I was at university four years prior to my homecoming, it felt poignant and melancholy. The original New Yorker cover shows people dining in the Bethesda Fountain in Central Park. Of course, when I saw the fountain, I immediately remembered the 2000s-era fountain in the Botanical Gardens. I traded the diners in for children doing homework, music practice, science experiments, and other academic (albeit wackily depicted) activities. I wanted to suggest that Hong Kong kids have academic excellence and competitiveness so deeply drilled into them that, even in bright, colourful, carefree settings — like splashing around in a park fountain — they'll still do homework. In the poem, I describe and allude to my personal experience of redefining my identity once my disability stopped me from achieving my career goals. The poem is a meditation on a person's value when their productivity is stunted.

FOUNTAIN OF YOUTH 青春之泉 • Children do homework and extracurricular activities in the now-renovated fountain of the Hong Kong Zoological and Botanical Gardens. Based on the July 18, 1988 New Yorker magazine cover by John O'Brien.

THE HONG KONGER ANTHOLOGY

> how is it scary to trick or treat
> in america when you know
> everyone gives out candy
> and doesn't question a ghost
> standing outside their door
> all of four-foot-two
> accompanied by a witch
> and a homemade pikachu
> isn't the thrill to knock on a door
> and be none the wiser
> if you'll find someone ready to feed
> or a confused local miser
> who has no clue what's going on
> and in panic shoos and abhors
> sending us kids back into the lift
> to try our luck on other floors

Ding Dong is one of my fun and frivolous Hong Kongers that doesn't carry an agenda. I used to love Halloween as a kid and would rock up to school in homemade costumes — Merlin, one of the 101 Dalmatians, Charlie Chaplin, a papier-mâché bobble-head Shrek (to name a few). I always tried to dress in costumes that no one else would have. I remember one year *everyone* was Harry Potter, another year in which *everyone* was a Pokémon character, and you could expect every year a smattering of Japanese cartoon characters would rock up to school. In *Ding Dong*, I reflected on all these Halloween memories. I wanted to celebrate these characters that I feel don't get represented on 31ˢᵗ October anymore in the 2020s. I also wanted to convey that homemade and childlike element of Halloween costume design where children and their parents craft elastic band Pikachu tails and Hello Kitty cat ear headbands. For the poem, I reflected on another Halloween experience which was trick-or-treating in the New Territories village that I grew up and still live in. Our village was part expat, part local. To this day we have a traditional Village Chief and there are local families who have lived in the same houses, passed down for generations. These families obviously did not grow up celebrating the pagan carnage of Halloween, and I remember that during the first Halloween we trick-or-treated in our village, our band of juvenile misfits deeply confused an old Chinese man who answered his door and was peer-pressured into offering our gaggle a handful of obscure boiled sweets.

SOPHIA HOTUNG

DING DONG 叮噹 • Children dressed as Doraemon, Hello Kitty, Ultraman, and Pikachu trick-or-treat in their apartment building. Based on the November 1, 1958 New Yorker magazine cover *Halloween* by William Steig.

47

THE HONG KONGER ANTHOLOGY

we'll come out before the sun
fresh from our desks
where drills keep us until five

man-lok will bring the air pump
sai-tong has a ball
i have half a gatorade

the girls with their instagrams
won't arrive 'til ten
but we don't have hours to play

taichi gonggongs and popos
will leave half a court
for a small one-sided game

how can we make the big leagues
with photographers
and martial artists treading

on the small rectangle court
we barely command
hidden behind rainbow blocks

Choi Hung depicts children playing basketball on courts of the eponymous housing estate in Kowloon. The poem comes from a young schoolboy and resident of Choi Hung Estate engaged in a turf war with elderly taichi neighbours and Instagram tourists. The piece contemplates the limited time and space afforded to Hong Kong students, specifically local students. In the poem, the children lack the time to play basketball for hours, and yet even if they did have time, the space would be shared or unavailable to them. The haiku form lent itself to that sense of restraint, due to its strict line and syllable count. In basketball, urban planning, and Hong Kong schooling, there also seems to be a sense of rigidity and structure.

SOPHIA HOTUNG

CHOI HUNG 氣貫長虹 • Children shoot hoops on Choi Hung Estate's basketball courts in Kowloon. Based on the May 29, 2017 New Yorker magazine cover *Brooklyn Bridge Park* by Jorge Colombo.

before they built the train and the water slides
before there were tokens per ride and a hotel on-site
we would pool our funds and arrive at ten
make our way straight to the cars

scale the highlands
on rusting wires
wondering who walked
the trail below
teetering over a swimming pool
a country club
a tennis court
four ships of boxed cargo

the idylls of a perch so high
waving at passing bubbles
any minute one could drop
and crash down on the rocks
we jostled for a red one
we jostled for the green
we'd end up in a purple
and hang hopes on the return

the raucous rides roll past the seahorse
etched into the grass
the mine train abyss
dragon eagle raging river
crazy galleon middle kingdom
atoll reef divers show

we keep the names inside our throats
and when we fly abroad
we call the rides at six flags
and disney these old names

we luncheon at mcdonald's
lose money tossing rings
and try to reach the cable cars
aboard the flying swings

Cable Guys triggers a sense of nostalgia that I felt upon learning that Ocean Park was scrapping my favourite rides, shifting from a ticket system to a token system, and installing a water park. My mother grew up with a water park version of Ocean Park and it made me think of growing up in Hong Kong as some cyclical loop. The generations before and after me will have "water park Ocean Park" and my grandchildren's generation and I will have "ride-centric Ocean Park". Circles therefore were on my mind when I created *Cable Guys*. I used a rounded brush for the whole piece and focused on curves with no hard edges or angles. Three boys peer out at a section of Ocean Park that was built once I had left Hong Kong to go to college. It's a reflection of my curmudgeonly wariness of change and my fixation on the erasure of childhood.

CABLE GUYS 高朋滿座 • Children peer out of an Ocean Park cable car and behold the fun of the fair below. Based on the September 5, 1964 New Yorker cover *New York World's Fair* by Arthur Kimmig Getz.

THE HONG KONGER ANTHOLOGY

> bucket hair beauty
> gizzard hair boy
> yeezy neon foam soles
> double sim card toy
> noise cancelling necklace
> tyrant cancelling zeal
> eco conscious fashion
> vegan conscious meal
> tiktok ban tan tunic
> red dye streak bleach locks
> thrift store suede heeled mules
> ten-toe carved out socks
> they text sans reservation
> yet never take calls
> no ice half sugar
> double tapioca balls

Bubble Teens is rooted in my fascination with Generation Z. The oldest Generation Z kids are said to be born in 1995. I was born in 1994 but repeated two years of school on account of being ill, meaning I grew up among Millennials but came of age among Gen Z-ers. I find Gen Z fascinating and feel that while I am close to many, I don't hold the same values, experiences, or chutzpah. Gen Z-ers' willingness to wear 2000s fashion, their gung-ho abrasiveness, and their selfie-savviness all contrast greatly against my reluctance to ever wear anything I wore in the 2000s, my self-effacing people-pleasing, and inability to take a nice photo of myself. All this floated around in my brain as I crafted the print and poem for *Bubble Teens*, both of which reflect some of the more amusing traits of Hong Kong Gen Z teens based on conversations with friends and posts from "Subtle Asian" Facebook groups.

SOPHIA HOTUNG

BUBBLE TEENS 珍珠奶茶 • A Generation Z couple enjoy a bubble tea date. Based on the August 8, 1925 New Yorker magazine cover by Julian de Miskey.

THE HONG KONGER ANTHOLOGY

i am but a child
no larger than a postage stamp
yet they fling me to the side
and stay home on the other

i grow up with strangers
wide-eyed loud-voiced ones
and nostalgia yearns for time
not a place one can revisit

the boarding pass the carry-on
extra weight luggage fee trapped in skies
onyxian black they make graves shallow
while sulphurous voices tin down beneath

and now my who-ness is the gulf
a shallow strait of what i have missed
i over here on green and pleasant land
my main land far away homeland to dust

Time Difference originally stemmed from the homesickness I felt aged 11 when I went to boarding school in England. I felt like my life had been sectioned into weekly chunks of confinement and freedom. I'd cry down a payphone at my mother for 15 weeks in exchange for three weeks of holiday. Every time I returned home, I felt that Hong Kong had changed. I was homesick not just for a place but for a place locked in 2005. In this print, I wanted to capture that feeling of separation and isolation, not just from a faraway home but for a bygone time. Creating *Time Difference*, I reflected on how the 2019 protests serve as a marker in Hong Kong's identity, a point of no return that functions similarly to how my departure to boarding school marked an ending during my childhood. The poem is adapted from Yu Guangzhong's *Nostalgia*. I wanted to use a Chinese poem given the protests' links to the Mainland, but I wanted the poem to focus less on politics and more on how processing political upheaval shapes children's identities. The poem also adopts a phrase from William Blake's *Jerusalem*, which was my boarding school's anthem. It references "England's green and pleasant land". Blake's poem felt significant given that *Jerusalem* critiques another type of revolution: the 19th century industrial revolution in Britain.

SOPHIA HOTUNG

TIME DIFFERENCE 打個電話返屋企 ● A boarding school student in England video calls his family as they take part in a pro-democracy protest. Based on the April 6, 2020 New Yorker magazine cover *Bedtime* by Chris Ware.

THE HONG KONGER ANTHOLOGY

mark my words
it is a fine thing to live in peace
where the streets are cleaned and walls are painted
roads are cleared of bricks and cairns
babes are home by sundown black
and dissidents take to chairs

where books are bound to burn in brains
safe there from trepidation
where hotel guests pin post-it notes
count fortnight-long vacations

where i look across at lands so proud
that no one can but ask
why kneel why dox why cancel why sue
why jab why protest why mask

the idyll of a pastorale
where choice is left to spies
who unburden you of decision fatigue
and instead harmonise

[Redacted] swapped the books depicted behind the girl in the original New Yorker cover with television screens. My spring senior seminar at university was called *Utopias & Dystopias*, and my thesis ended up being a novel: a George Orwell parody of *Nineteen Eighty-Four*, called *2018*. The novel begins with the protagonist, an alt-right Columbia student, studying in Butler Library. I had a serious chronic illness relapse that put me in hospital and kept me from my finals during my senior fall semester. I had to take all my final exams in one day as soon as I got back to campus the following semester, and I remember being jetlagged, studying at 5am in an empty reading room in Butler Library, much like the girl in *[Redacted]*. When I made the print, therefore, I was recreating that memory. The screens all depict elements of Chinese industrial and economic development. They are real photos from news reports showing cargo ships coming into port, Covid-19 vaccine development, military parades, galactic sojourns, and so on. The girl, meanwhile, reads from an old book that is barely legible after having so much of it redacted. The print and its corresponding poem hint at the 2010s-era apathy that certain Hong Kongers feel towards China's growth and development. In the poem, you may pick up on references to the 2019 protests and Hong Kong's austere 14- to 21-day Covid-19 quarantine protocols.

[REDACTED] 和諧 • A student studies a highly redacted text in a dingy library while televisions blare around her. Based on the March 3, 1973 New Yorker magazine cover by Arthur Kimmig Getz.

i know my mum was hot once
i've seen sepia photos
of her with dad bikinily-clad
exploring lantau grottos
when did she get naggy
why's she now a bummer
who goes and hires air force flyers
to thwart my hot girl summer

Hot Girl Bummer is a pun on "Hot Girl Summer", the 2019 phenomenon popularised by the American rapper Megan Thee Stallion. I wanted to contrast the differences between that stereotypical, cool, western "mom" who's your friend (think Regina George's mother in the 2004 teen movie, *Mean Girls*), and that classic trope of the bossy, over-bearing, Asian mum (think the mother in Just Kidding Films' 2012 YouTube sketch, *Shit Asian Moms Say* — I actually based the drawing of the mother in this print on that matriarch). To devise the messages overhead, I crowdsourced real text messages from friends' Hong Kong mothers. (My own mother is too Eurasian to be an overtly bossy, overbearing mother so my own texts from her weren't very helpful for this exercise.) The text messages, I think, show the sexism and colourism that some of Hong Kong's Gen X women have internalised about what it means to be chaste or fair-skinned. In fact, the original text of "Do not get so tan" was "do not get so dark", but I felt that "tan" got the message across clearly enough without me writing explicitly racist messages across the sky. The poem delves into the hypocrisy of the mother's commands, while also being one of my shorter, fun poems to read aloud at your next inter-generational Sunday dinner.

SOPHIA HOTUNG

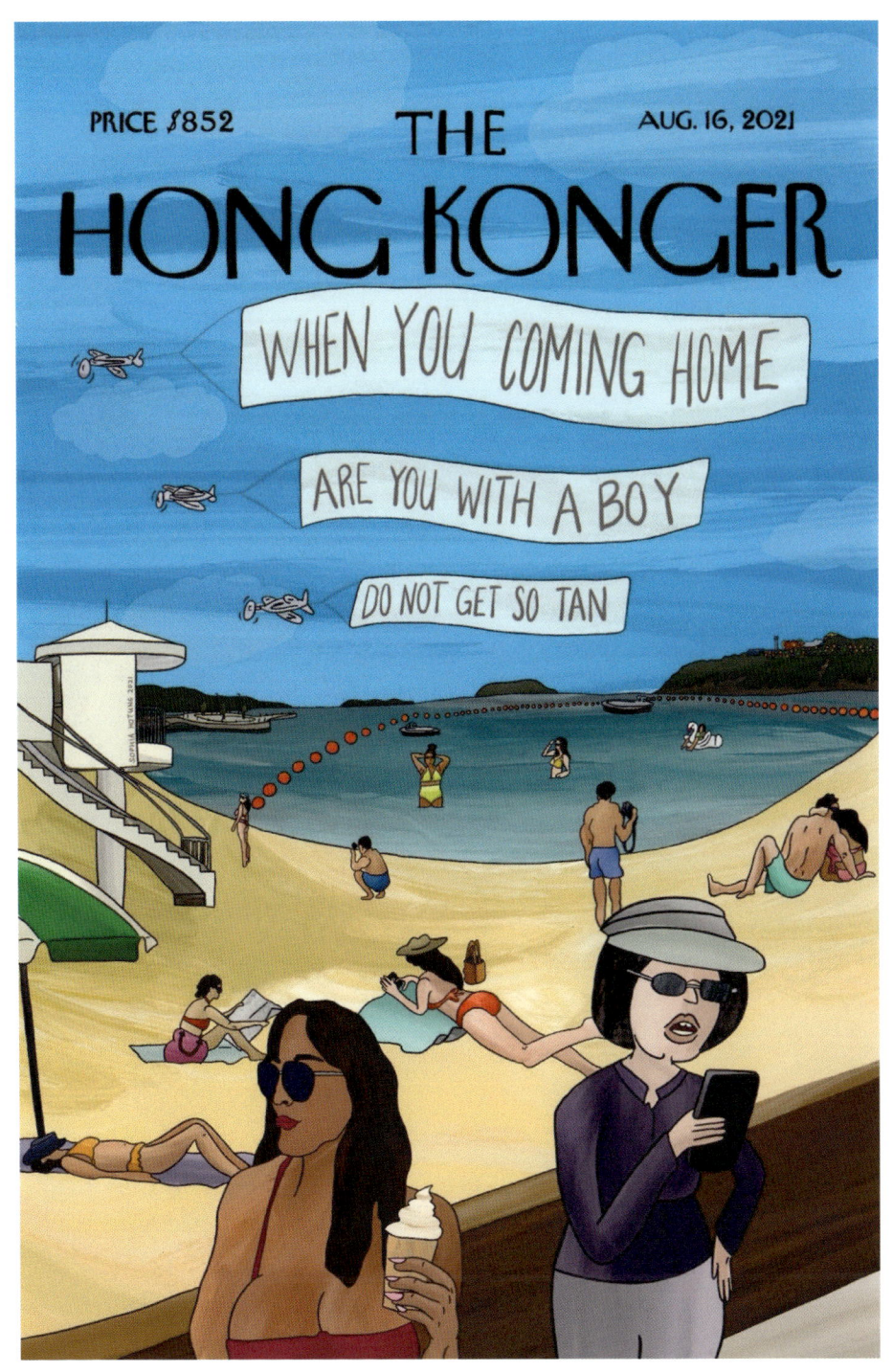

HOT GIRL BUMMER 天理難容 • Plane banners soar over sunbathing and canoodling beachgoers on Repulse Bay Beach, delivering messages from an anxious mother. Based on the August 16, 2021 New Yorker magazine cover *Hi It's Mom* by Roz Chast.

THE HONG KONGER ANTHOLOGY

> i came for a drink and stayed for a night
> 'til they peeled me off the bonnet
> of a taxi on wyndham
> i made a wager that went sour
> took in a balcony brawl
> then hid in the smoke with a turk and a girl
> who badmouthed the suits with their vapes and their weed
> above us the thudding of synth and ket
> exchanged mouths pushed by tongues on the lilac star air
> and the sour of whiskey burned deep down the line
> to the guilt of a conman and the tears of a sinner
> so resolved in my filth i allowed myself grace
> and sat back in a chair with ass in my face
> and as the sun brought to mind that i'd be called to my desk
> i came out to greet it and expel my mess

LKF, which stands for Lan Kwai Fong, a popular expat bar district south of Central, illustrated the vertical nature of nightlife in Hong Kong. The building could be in Wan Chai or Tsim Sha Tsui too, two other bar districts. The Chinese name for the print is an idiom which can be read as "being confined to a small area but completely whole". The first character, 五, also means "five", signifying the five floors of this particular building. Overall, the Chinese title and the print's poem emphasise that in Hong Kong you could have a whole night out in one building: starting off playing pool, getting into a bar brawl, smoking shisha, chatting with friends, hopping into an EDM mosh-pit, hooking up, doing shots, calling your ex, watching a strip show, then vomiting off a balcony. The poem recounts the speaker's activities as he drifts up the building and through the floors. A secondary reading of the poem implies that the speaker not only vomits off the top floor balcony but also falls entirely off himself, ending up having to be "peeled off the bonnet of a taxi" below. Morbid but it's printed now. Sorry.

LKF 五臟俱全 • An average Lan Kwai Fong building on a Saturday night, housing a hookah bar, nightclub, bar, strip club, and their assorted patrons. Based on the June 25, 2018 New Yorker magazine cover *City Living* by Harry Bliss.

o what can ail thee chad mcgee
alone and pale and loitering
your amex glistens like the jewel
on your college signet ring

i met a lady at the bar
full beautiful an exotic child
her hair was long her ass was tight
and her eyes were tired

i ordered drinks paid the tab
veuve and dom on ice
i looked at her and willed a kiss
a peck would have sufficed

i bundled her inside a cab
and paid to drive all night long
but sideways she would turn
and retch a lipgloss ethyl pong

i took her to my condo's roof
and there she moaned her feet were sore
i tried to close her tired tired eyes
she thought i was fifty i'm thirty-four

she held out 'til i fell asleep
and there i dreamed she'd stayed the night
the longest dream i'd ever had
'til i woke choking on my side

my starved lips hurled from futoned floor
with loss my loins gaped bereft
i fumbled and found she'd disappeared
no note to leave before she'd left

and this is why i lurk out here
alone and pale and loitering
these girls don't know a nice guy
when he's flashing her with his thing

Cupidity continues the theme of nightlife, this time focusing on "yellow fever" (a phrase that refers to the fetishisation of Asian women usually by white men) and incel culture (which stands for "involuntary celibate", an online collective of men who are unable to procure girlfriends despite feeling that they are "nice guys". Spoiler: 99.999% of them are not nice guys). I set the scene at the Armani / Privē bar in Chater House, which recently closed. I remember once going there with a gaggle of awkward 17- and 18-year-old friends to see what it was like. It was glitzy and expensive but felt like a place you'd take a girl to show off your American Express card. The poem is based on John Keats's *La Belle Dame Sans Merci*, a poem I see as a case study for the male gaze. I interpret the poem as a man in love with a woman who he cannot see is repulsed by him. *Cupidity*'s poem, therefore, touches upon the pressure that women feel to accommodate people who make them uncomfortable and sneak out of potentially dangerous situations so as not to anger men and thereby endanger themselves.

SOPHIA HOTUNG

CUPIDITY 愛語尼 • A gawky expat fawns over his disinterested date at the Armani/Privé terrace in Central. Based on the February 19, 1996 New Yorker magazine cover *Cupid's Volley* by Peter de Sève.

there was a café north of elgin street
that served hot chocolate and acai bowls
and walking home from work at six
i found it light for a night in september

two laptops clackered in my pack
one for audit one for me
i cracked the latter open and started
pen to paper finger to key

from there i'd write and make a mug last
'til darkness turned me out to the street
i could picture the headlines across the gazettes
info risk analyst pens the next sensation

back home i watch them glide
up the hill travellating to hot meals and soft beds
all things i have instead of a plume
all things i savour before making a jump

over noodles and packet sauce
i sit in my window and eat from the pan
starving for applause that does not come
for my hot desk cfa big four career

Happy Hour is based on my time in Edinburgh where I briefly worked as a graduate trainee IT auditor after leaving university. Hours weren't long and during the first month of my employment, I would clock out just after 5pm and stop by a coffee shop on my walk home to write my novel, watching through the window as people commuted from work themselves. For *Happy Hour*, I relocated the subject of this print to a coffee shop on Lyndhurst Terrace, watching commuters glide up Shelley Street after work. When I worked in IT audit and later in crisis communications and business development, I thought a lot about how I could finesse a leap between having a respectable, income-generating career, and actualising my juvenile dreams of authordom. I did not write consistently; I did not submit to publications regularly; I did not solicit literary agents at all, but I did hang on to the hope that one day I'd get "discovered". Sometimes I think about how my disability's annihilation of my corporate career was a good thing: I only started creating art for a living because there was nothing else that I could do from bed. Of course, my parents' financial support was the true facilitator, funding my medical treatments, allowing me to move back home to avoid rent, gifting me an iPad for Christmas — I think a lot about my financial privilege and whether or not my success has been due to money or myself. It's an uncomfortable topic of conversation and one that only gets thornier when disability, race, and gender intersect with it. I don't have an answer for what my behaviour and approach should be to account for my privilege, but for now, I'm just trying not to get sicker and trying not to be Veruca Salt.

SOPHIA HOTUNG

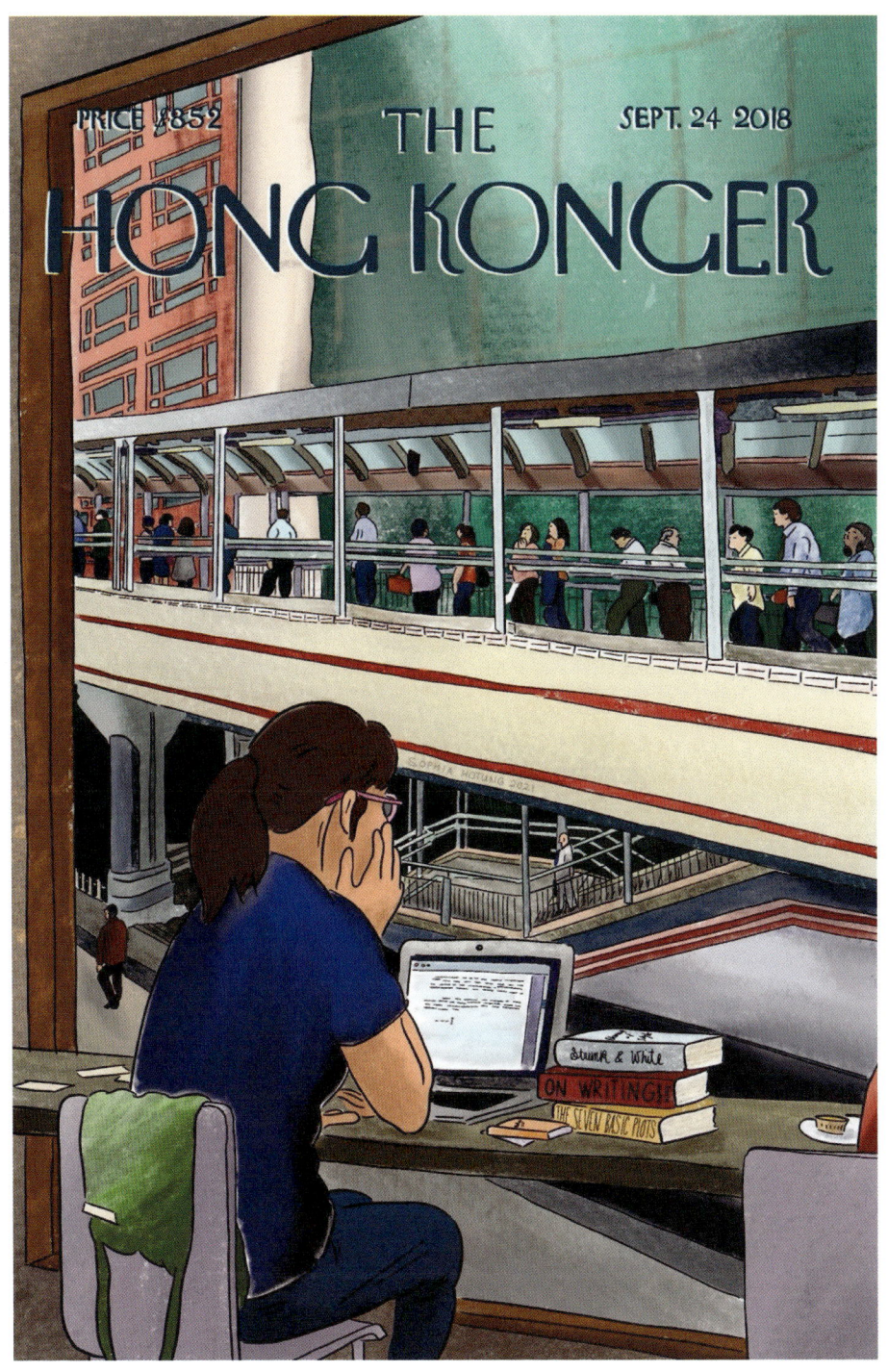

HAPPY HOUR 攀壁偷光 • A young writer works on her novel after work as Central commuters ride the Mid-levels escalator home. Based on the September 24, 2018 New Yorker magazine cover *Fourth Wall* by Adrian Tomine.

i could not stop the world from ringing in my ears
from pulling at my sinews and gnawing at my bones
men eat of fame and die men clutch at fame and fall
but the bustle in a house the morning after a shaven life
holds down its off button until the machine goes cold
and the powers that be hover to press it again
the whir of the unit and the twinkling monitor light
must feel like cold water to the microchip brain
rapid eye movement along a random access memory
unreliable and forgetful with a full scratch disk
i could not stop the world and i could not stop myself
for we are two fighting a struggle enough in an empty room
but why repeal the beating ground when you can put
your ear to it and let the pulse resonate through your ribs
its beat spurring your wrists to write and fingers to curl
mouth to move and lungs to sing

Extra Extra was created during a low-point of creating this anthology. Originally, I crowdsourced to create a book of the Hong Konger prints alongside relevant anecdotes and interviews. Some submissions that I received were insightful and powerful, so much so that they made me realise that one page was not going to do their content justice. However, other submissions led me to conversations that turned me into a counsellor, secretary, or punching bag. Strangers told me that I had no right appropriating Hong Kong culture as a white-passing person; others wanted me to create new Hong Konger prints because they did not feel that any of my current prints paired well with what they had to say; it became clear halfway through some interviews that my subjects were primarily focused on promoting their brands rather than engaging with Hong Kong issues. Three months into trying to curate a book with meaningful stories and experiences from Hong Kongers, I felt stuck and browbeaten. I found it difficult to maintain my voice and direction with people telling me that I was too white, too privileged, or too young to know how to pull together this book. I took a break from liaising with interview contacts and went back to square one. I returned to the art, which I had not been able to do for a while given the research work. During this moment, I made *Extra Extra*. When people meet me, I'm usually high-energy and enthusiastic, cracking jokes and making faces. I think it's because I want to put people at ease and want to start off relationships assuming the best. However, I am always thinking about my disability: how it could rear its head any minute and debilitate me during a friendly chat or a high-stakes moment. The print's newspaper kiosk is colourful and vibrant to reflect my outward friendliness, but my face in *Extra Extra* is, like my insides, overwhelmed and exhausted. I don't think my outward versus inward attitudes are unique. I think most people put on a show for others while being sad or fed-up on the inside. During this reflective phase, I realised the whole reason that I decided to make a Hong Konger book was because I had all these thoughts about each Hong Konger print. I considered writing fake narratives about the characters in them, but some Hong Konger prints were too serious for that. Then I thought I could write straightforward histories of things like reservoirs and marriage equality, but that felt dry. I landed on writing poetry because it allows you to be pensive, serious, and silly within a consistent form. I also included these artist's notes because I realised that to do the Hong Kongers justice, the stories behind creating each one needed to be mentioned. At the end of the day, by crafting poems and artist's notes, I was reassuring myself that my perspective was enough and that I did not have to be at the beck and call of others to be or create something meaningful. The poem borrows phrases from various Emily Dickinson poems like *Fame is a Fickle Food* and *The Bustle in a House*. Being an introverted hermit, I felt a kinship with Dickinson, who spent most of her life alone, only talking to people through letters, which is what I've had to do (but with texts and emails), given my immobility.

SOPHIA HOTUNG

EXTRA EXTRA 出來行 • The artist sits alone in a newsagent's kiosk, surrounded by her Hong Konger magazines. Based on the May 30, 1931 New Yorker magazine cover *News Stand* by Barney Tobey.

67

the drives up to the places
where leaves were not swept
and boar and mongooses ran
we would see rocks in forms
of lions and amahs
crawling under them through tunnels
navigating cairns and winding roads
until we came to grassland and rice fields
and in the wide eyes of a child self
i imagined a day in the distant future
when i would climb to the top and overlook
a city i owned

but now i cannot climb
and i do not own the city
the wheels on the chair do not roll on
jagged rocks and the balls of the cane
do not balance on boulders
so i drive through the tunnel
and i watch from the dirt
and wonder if they'll ever build a world
that lets me up

Lion Rock Station is actually a print I made out of frustration with the Mid-Levels escalators, although most people view it as a comment on nature conservation and the expansion of the MTR northwards into China. There is a sign by the elevator for the escalators on Lyndhurst Terrace that politely informs wheelchair users that they are welcome to use the lift, but there is not another one on the other side. In short, don't use the lift if you plan on getting off at any point on the escalator other than the point you started at. As a kid, my family used to drive up to Beas River to pet horses and behold grass by passing through the Lion Rock Tunnel and by Amah's Rock. My Popo would tell us the legend behind Amah's Rock and point out the nose, mane, and jaw of the Lion. An avid hiker herself, she told us that Lion Rock was especially hard to climb, but promised that when we were older, she would take us. We never went, Popo is now gone, and I can't climb Shelley Street without the escalator. *Lion Rock Station*, therefore, was my attempt at creating an accessible path to the top of Lion Rock, but with Hong Kong being Hong Kong, I ensured that when I got to the concourse of my new Lion Rock MTR station, there would be no elevator up to the exit... only stairs. Wheelchair users could very well get to Lion Rock Station, but they'd never be able to ascend to Lion Rock itself. The poem deals more with my Popo's role in this backstory and the sense of loss that disability inevitably incurs.

SOPHIA HOTUNG

LION ROCK STATION 獅子山上 • A property developer exits a new MTR station built atop Lion Rock Hill. Based on the August 5, 2002 New Yorker magazine cover by Eric Drooker.

THE HONG KONGER ANTHOLOGY

> muimui at the banquet
> lording over the cheek squeezers
> mouth breathers cough wheezers
> peekaboo teasers old geezers
> spoonfulling egg custard abalone glop
> a gnarled chicken foot waits in the soupy abyss
> eyeing her disdain mr fish gapes and gawps
> a sprig of scallion locked in his teeth
> the chicken skin goosepimples as if it had been cold
> waiting for death in the abattoir
> the flesh and the sinew and cartilage lumps
> are from body parts not taught at school
> the red bean too thick too sweet for legumes
> the egg drops too sticky the tripe too hard chewed
> while popo devours the regurgitants with zeal
> muimui ponders on happier meals

Bao Bei's Feast was inspired by a Chinese banquet I attended as a child. I must have been seven or eight, and my elder sister and I were sipping broth in an umpteen-course meal at the Summer Palace restaurant in the Island Shangri-La. Our mother sat next to us. We were being tactful, tiny diners until, horrified, we found severed chicken feet, curled and goosepimpled, at the bottom of our bowls. I was terrified to eat any more but felt that I was proving to everyone that I could not connect with my Chinese heritage because I could not stomach Chinese food. Now, as an adult, I have coeliac disease. It has no cure or treatment, so to manage it, all I can do is abstain from gluten, which is in most Chinese food in the form of wheat, soy sauce, barley, malt, and other things that normal people don't think about. *Bao Bei's Feast* shows a Eurasian toddler thinking about a Happy Meal with a feast of Chinese delicacies set out before her. It's a nod to my sense of shame of not only disliking tripe and abalone but also of not being able to eat tripe and abalone as a coeliac. I wanted to keep the poem childlike and fun with a strong rhyming structure and rhythm. I reference my Popo in the final line about the "regurgitant". Popo grew up in Shanghai and experienced famine, leaving for Hong Kong only just in time to escape the Japanese invasion. She ate everything and anything, chewing chicken wings down to the bone, even as a 70-year-old retiree in Surrey. One time when we visited her, one of us grandkids left a regurgitated morsel of gristle on their plate. She reached out, chopsticked it, and popped it in her mouth. We were all horrified but contextually, it was symbolic of how out-of-touch all five of her grandkids had become compared to her own upbringing and childhood. In all, the poem and artwork seek to reflect the connection to Chinese heritage that all five of us cousins on my maternal side have each lost to some degree.

SOPHIA HOTUNG

PRICE $852   THE   Feb. 17, 1973

HONG KONGER

BAO BEI'S FEAST 小皇帝綜合症 • A Eurasian toddler can only crave a McDonald's Happy Meal despite the Chinese banquet spread out before her. Based on the February 17, 1973 New Yorker magazine cover *The New Yorker Cat Feast Cover* by Ronald Searle.

onward to lethe i fought not to go
twisting and rooting myself in poisons
suffering my pale forehead to burn
cutting out nightshades grains legumes
jerking from pharma to rosary to yoga
alone in my sorrow's mysteries
too drowsy now to shade and shy away
my wakeful anguish drowned out warnings
that to the herbalist i trudged
though 'twas as if hemlock i had drunk
i forced the goblet still
snakes and sharks and turtle shells
ground and brewed and imbibed
to glut my sorrow and rise with morning
only wobbled my bones and frayed my veins
i dwelt in bed where i made to die
rich with anger imprisoned in pillows
feeding deep deep upon oils and chalks
my ancestors promised would relieve
turning to poison with bee-stung lips
red raw and cracked and burning
seeing no relief none saving me
only scalding my palate and loosening my teeth
only poisoning me more among my cloudy trophies
i cannot hang a rosette that i am cured how they were

Pharmacist's New Yorker counterpart shows a baker showcasing her buns, croissants, and loaves. As a coeliac who can't eat gluten, that wasn't going to vibe with me, so we had to change up the goods. Chinese medicine is an iffy point of conversation for me. I've had chronic illnesses — many of which are digestive — for over ten years, and nothing gets people recommending seahorse skeleton paste and dragon scrotum tea more than having a chronic, digestive problem in Hong Kong. Surprisingly, none of these balms and brews have ever cured or helped me, though they have left me poorer or keeled over clutching my gut. Like with *Bao Bei's Feast*, I sometimes feel that I am so disconnected from my Chinese heritage that my ancestors' medicine does not cure me. Nonsense, I know, but I do wonder if sometimes it's not the medicine but me — I'm imbibing the elixir wrong or maybe I misunderstood the instructions. The poem is another Keatsian adaptation, this one of *Ode to Melancholy*, with the "hemlock" line poached from *Ode to a Nightingale*. I like Keats when he's not being lascivious because, like Emily Dickinson and me, he was cooped up in bed a lot sick (he had tuberculosis). He even died from it at 26, which was not lost on me, beginning this project at the ripe old age of 26.

SOPHIA HOTUNG

PHARMACIST 拾藥 • A traditional Chinese medicine shopkeeper mans the cash register. Based on the November 11, 1974 New Yorker magazine cover by Laura Jean Allen.

careful it's hot
here hold it on the side
oh that's lovely presentation
is that a yolk running
a mayonnaise i make
there's a special ingredient
what is that chives
coriander
exotic
the pork is braised
these are strong spices
i will show you how to stomach it
with hp sauce and salad cream

Baps & Baos is also about my maternal grandparents. The Bap Man symbolises Grandpa Lawrie and the Bao Lady symbolises Popo. They met working for the Hong Kong government and had children during a time when Eurasian halfies were still rare. Grandpa Lawrie was famous for his steak and kidney-less (nobody liked kidney) pies and Popo was famous for clay pot chicken, "Popo's cabbage", and glass fensi noodles. The depiction of them sharing food from their respective cultures with the new Legislative Council building behind them was a rose-tinted view of their marriage creating a cultural bridge despite their differences. The poem, however, is darker. It functions as a dialogue between the Bap Man and Bao Lady, though it's not always clear who is speaking. The characters in the poem interrupt, patronise, and misunderstand one another, all with an air of faux friendliness. I did not necessarily want to expose conflict within my grandparents' relationship, but rather highlight the fake smiles and patronising comments that seem to be inherent in all cross-cultural exchanges.

BAPS & BAOS 文化交流 • A food truck cook exchanges a British sandwich for a Chinese dumpling in front of the Legislative Council Complex in Tamar Park. Based on the April 9, 2018 New Yorker magazine cover *Gluten-Free Gluten* by Bruce McCall.

folks bade us adieu and sent us west to the yellow crane towers
amid sand dunes and particle dust we watch and wait with phantom limbs from planes
the faraway ghost of a lonely jet dissolves in the smog's own void
so we breathe in the harbour and trace its waters to the edge of the city and sky

Afternoon Tea shows a young family eating childhood snacks, like bolobao and Kowloon Dairy chocolate milk, while looking out onto the construction of the Kai Tak Development, which promises to be a new residential hub and an answer to Hong Kong's housing crisis. I drive along the Kwun Tong Bypass often in real life, passing Kai Tak and the herd of cranes that populate it. There is an ancient landmark in Wuhan called the Yellow Crane Tower. It's given a lot of airtime in Chinese poetry, including in Li Bai's poem, *Seeing Off Meng Haoran for Guangling at Yellow Crane Tower*. Given the yellow cranes that clutter the up-and-coming Kai Tak Development area of Kowloon Bay and the nature of young couples starting families and leaving the nest (pun unintended), I parodied Li Bai's poem, changing certain words to reflect coming of age as a Millennial in Hong Kong. Mine is the last generation to remember colonial Hong Kong with its Kai Tak Airport runway or coins with Queen Elizabeth II's head on them. Now, we face a housing crisis that forces many young adults to live at home until they have families of their own. I made the parents in *Afternoon Tea* consume children's snacks and drinks to imply that members of our generation can be so financially stunted that, in many ways, such as by living at home, we are still children despite some of us being parents ourselves.

SOPHIA HOTUNG

AFTERNOON TEA 下午茶 • A couple enjoys teatime with their dog and toddler, overlooking the land reclamation of Kai Tak and Kowloon Bay. Based on the August 31, 2015 New Yorker magazine cover *Gowanus Canal, Brooklyn* by Adrian Tomine.

think of it this way did you know
the average household spends
four per cent of monthly income
cleaning and making mends
but with a thirteen square foot flat
think how you'll be saving
no more soap expenditure
that's something you'll be craving

think of it this way did you know
the average couple pays
8,000 dollars every week
supporting kids say surveys
but with a half-bedroom paradise
think of what you'll be saving
no more brats that pee the bed
that's something you'll be craving

think of it this way did you know
the average person wastes
half their life fighting a spouse
that strife could be erased
yes with a place not built for two
in fact just built for one
trade in your spouse for this idyllic house
and live twice as long just alone

Penthouse is an unsubtle contrast piece between Hong Kong's notorious "cage homes" and extortionate housing prices of apartments that should not be so extortionately priced. The poem stems from the perspective of the overzealous, neon, eighties-inspired real estate agent, doing her best to upsell a pricey apartment in an "up-and-coming" neighbourhood to a down-to-earth couple. In the New Yorker original, there is a sliver of a view of the Hudson River between two buildings, but I figured that this is Hong Kong, where the housing situation is a little more dire. There's no view here.

SOPHIA HOTUNG

PENTHOUSE 近山漏水 • An overzealous real estate agent shows off a disappointing view from a disappointing balcony of a disappointing flat to a hopeful couple. Based on the June 11, 2001 New Yorker magazine cover *End of the Line* by Peter de Sève.

THE HONG KONGER ANTHOLOGY

steal the ice
lure the fish
up to the surface where there is air
mine the rock
pocket the ore
toss it from the foreman's post
walk with little air between
your soles and the unsalted slate
for floodlight pounces with little warning
and sends men sinking
through the portals they carved

After Hours harks back to the popular Hong Kong childhood pastime of ice skating. I don't know why Hong Kong is so into ice skating. Maybe being cold is such a novelty that it's become an industry. In any case, I feel that any Hong Kong kid who was anyone had an ice-skating birthday party (I never did). The print's Chinese name, 偷雞摸魚, literally translates into "to steal chicken and pilfer fish". It's an idiom that describes thievery and illicit behaviour. In *After Hours*, a Zamboni driver is returning to his workplace to ice-fish in the dead of night. It's a comment on employer-employee relationships and worker exploitation in Hong Kong. Respect for authority is deeply ingrained into Chinese Confucian culture. Speaking up against one's loban or boss is considered taboo; conversely, subservience and loyalty are rewarded. However, the pandemic, protests, and western influence have led to changes in attitudes towards employers for a younger generation of workers who have adopted more individualistic values of work-life balance and seek work schedules that allow more for a life outside of the office. The poem villainises the Confucian belief system of acquiescence: the speaker encourages the Zamboni driver to literally 摸魚 or "pilfer fish". However, the final lines of the poem warn that hubris and entitlement can lead the pilfering Zamboni driver to his just desserts, falling through ice that he neglected to maintain properly.

SOPHIA HOTUNG

AFTER HOURS 偷冰摸魚 • A Zamboni driver at Festival Walk's ice-skating rink sneaks onto the ice after hours for some fishing. Based on the February 3, 2003 New Yorker magazine cover by Bruce McCall.

i will come back to the falls
but i cannot say just when
i will leave dear guanyu here among
the cats and spidermen
under christ's blessing hand
raised to touch the poor
a ghostly face looks up at me
on the styxian floor
i did not come to deck the place
nor for the pawnshop cheque
i came with trust blind and lost
that these survive the wreck
i leave my worldly goods and loves
to dally in porcelain dwell
while bubble wrap and cardboard caves
convert our home to shell
i will come back to find my men
i pray for low winds there
while i strive to fix my lot
i entrust them to your care

10,000 Faeries is the only print with an English title that derives from its Chinese one, 萬仙陣. My friend Janice, who collaborated with me on interviews, came up with the idea to make a Hong Konger of the porcelain figurines at Waterfall Bay Park. The figurines at the park are mainly deities but on occasion, you can find a Jesus Christ figurine or even Spiderman. They sit, exposed to the elements, cared for by volunteer custodians. Janice and I found this print's original New Yorker cover while in a coffee shop and knew immediately to substitute the snowmen for figurines. I started working on *10,000 Faeries* while undergoing an experimental monoclonal antibody treatment, Rituximab, which successfully (and unexpectedly) improved my refractive autoimmune conditions. I received my first set of blood results that showed the treatment's effectiveness while sketching *10,000 Faeries*, so I called my partner Spencer and our mothers to tell them that the treatment had worked. When I hung up, I added Spencer, our mothers, Janice, her brother and the book's translator Sean, my caregivers Nora and Nick, and our two family dogs Sparky and Coco into the background of the print. If you zoom in, you can see the gang. The poem tells the story of a Hong Konger who has fallen on hard times and has had to move out of his home. He has moved his porcelain figurines to Waterfall Bay Park, hoping that they will be cared for there, so that when he returns, prosperous once more, he'll be able to collect them. It's a poem about loss, hope, and trusting the process. There are elements of Adrienne Rich's poem *Diving into the Wreck*, which was the first poem I ever studied at college. It's one of my favourite poems that I meditated on before writing this poem. It is also referenced more explicitly in *Junk of the Magi*.

SOPHIA HOTUNG

10,000 FAERIES 萬仙陣 • Porcelain figurines stand guard at Waterfall Bay Park. Based on the January 8, 1972 New Yorker magazine cover by Charles Samuel Addams.

THE HONG KONGER ANTHOLOGY

i do not love you except because i love you
i go from missing you to not remembering you're there
from waiting to not waiting for your key
in the lock of the door to feed me my dinner
i love you only because it's you the one i know
i hate you deeply for holding back the ball
and holding back the bowl and holding back the leash
and holding back your fist and boot when i don't bend to you
the measure of my love for you
is whole and pure and brief
it's that i do not see you
but love you through my grief

Weekday Warriors portrays real dogs from Hong Kong Dog Rescue's Instagram account, all except for the middle left-most pooch who was my dog, Gus. I wanted to celebrate mongrel village dogs that are quintessentially Hong Kong, common Chinese breeds like chow-chows and shar-peis, and imported breeds like huskies and German shepherds. I adapted an English translation of Pablo Neruda's Spanish poem *I Do Not Love You Except Because I Love You* as it feels like the perfect mantra for a pet dog. The print and its poem examine the psyche of pets left at home while their owners go to work, with the poem going further to touch upon unconditional love, even in the face of abuse.

SOPHIA HOTUNG

WEEKDAY WARRIORS 何日君再來 • Dogs peer from the windows of an apartment building while waiting for their owners to return home from work. Based on the August 13, 2007 New Yorker magazine cover by Mark Ulriksen.

my master cannot walk me
he works a six to nine
but he has come up with a way
that suits me almost fine

knowing dogs are nature's beasts
destined to roam outside
he dragged in a palm plant friend
for my soul to confide

knowing dogs are nature's beasts
keen to hike the hills
he hung up three ink-stained frames
of mountains and spoonbills

knowing dogs are nature's beasts
woofing in the wind
he cracked his window half
to blow back pollution

my master cannot see me
but i could go see him
out the window down the streets
to hunt his location

Room With a View takes its name from E.M. Forster's eponymous novel, which begins with 19th century British ladies complaining about the dull views from their Florence hotel rooms. The print did not start out as a critique of Hong Kong's drab, polluted apartment vistas, but — being one of the first Hong Kongers I ever started — it was an early attempt at taking New Yorker elements and translating them literally into Hong Konger ones. The teapot became bubble tea; the houseplant became a Dracaena Marginata; the black cat became a white mini poodle, and so on. I left the print for months to work on others, leaving it to become the sixth-to-last print that I finished for the book. When I returned to complete it, I was a seasoned pro at translating New Yorkers into Hong Kongers so delved deeper into exploring one's connection with nature when cooped up in a block of flats. I changed the apartment's interior, decorating it with orchids and that aforementioned spiky plant, Chinese brush paintings, and even a floral lamp. I then embedded the print's Chinese name and other tree-hugging chengyus (Chinese idioms) into the signage outside the window. You may have noticed that the Chinese title of the print is on the foregrounded chengyu, 滿目青山, but that its second character is misspelled as 自. The correct character, 目, can be translated into "eyes". I changed the 目 to 自 to highlight the irony of the chengyu 滿目青山 when it comes to this print. (滿目青山 means "greenery as far as the eye can see".) When it came to writing the poem, I did not reflect too much on nature but instead continued to explore *Weekday Warriors*' theme of pets when their masters are away. *Room With a View*'s poem is from the white mini poodle's point of view and examines its connection to nature from its seat in the apartment.

SOPHIA HOTUNG

THE HONG KONGER
PRICE $852 — Mar. 1, 1982

ROOM WITH A VIEW 滿目青山 • A white poodle waits for its owner to return home to their small studio apartment overlooking a Sham Shui Po street market. Based on the March 1, 1982 New Yorker magazine cover by Jean-Jacques Sempé.

i sent the kids to boarding school despite their moans and bawls
two went off to gordonstoun and one to beeston hall

it left me time to self-reflect and so i did my rounds
changed their rooms to studies gyms adopted myself three hounds

lola spike and dorothy all mutts with golden brows
the trainer taught them fervently to not defile the house

on sundays we took brusque brisk walks along the trailing heights
woofing laughing sniffing barking no teenage angst in sight

we cherish our time together willing not to be deflated
that when christmas comes my girls return from being incarcerated

Peak Trail does not have a significant meaning. I just thought it would look pretty good. I had thoughts to make the poem about the dog poisonings that have happened along Bowen Road and Black's Link since the 1990s, but in the end, I thought a scenario where a mother is more interested in her pets than her own children would be funny, and a little levity was required after two prints and poems about dogs feeling trapped.

SOPHIA HOTUNG

PRICE $852   THE   MAR. 11, 2019

THE HONG KONGER

PEAK TRAIL 呂洞賓嗖狗 • A woman walks her dogs along the Peak Trail. Based on the March 11, 2019 New Yorker magazine cover *Off the Path* by Gayle Kabaker.

89

THE HONG KONGER ANTHOLOGY

we were killing pigs when the americans arrived
a tuesday morning typhoon washed gutter blood
outside the wet market to nelson street
from a child we heard her squealing
then heard it stop as she caught view of us
in our gloves and aprons legs and hocks in hand
lines of glistening shoulders hanging
amah'ed perambulators and parasols
soft white hands and arms unworked unblamed
gagging for fusion not that we needed them
haggling low prices sheltering their babes
distracting them from our livelihoods with tubes of gelatin sweets

Pigs in Blankets was inspired by a story my mother tells of how, when she was a child, she and my aunt would complain to my Popo about going to the stinky, scary wet market. She now feels bad that she complained and indirectly snubbed her Chinese heritage. It's her version of the foot soup story I touched upon in *Bao Bei's Feast*. I wanted to create a morbid juxtaposition between the slabs of raw pork hanging in the background and lying in the stall with the baby-pink piglet stuffed toy that the girl in the push-chair is cuddling. The title thereby references the food that is "pigs in blankets", which are sausages rolled in pastry, and the literal piglet stuffed toy napping with the child. The poem adapts Seamus Heaney's *Anahorish 1944*, which is about American World War II soldiers manoeuvring past a slaughterhouse in Ireland. I kept the first line completely the same as the first line in Heaney's poem, except now the Americans aren't soldiers but expatriates who are making an effort to shop locally but are nevertheless horrified by the no-frills Hong Kong butchers. The mention of Nelson Street situates this wet market in Mong Kok.

PIGS IN BLANKETS 殺豬不見血 • A mother chats with a wet market butcher as her child slumbers in a push-chair, cuddling a stuffed toy pig that resembles the butcher's wares. Based on the May 30, 2011 New Yorker magazine cover *Small Growers* by Peter de Sève.

what does this rash look like should i go to
matilda our lovely helper/nanny will be available
from september back-to-school recommendations for
backpacks are becoming too heavy shall we petition
teachers to give less work from home opportunities for
a single mom whose child is this getting dragged along by
your helper bed wanted cannot find in ikea or wing on a
mission to save saltwater fish i've put in the sink with
tap water only asking for 10,000 signatures for my
daughter's oat milk petition the government to get
kids back to school tutor needed for my son in p2
his weak points are many people can i get to
share this post and raise awareness
of how much cheaper things
are in kowloon
is too far
please
suggest
shops in
central
where i
can look
for iherb code please thanks in advance

Hong Kong Moms is a satire of the infamous Facebook group comprising 65,100 members (at time of writing). Although the group is useful and riddled with mothers just trying to do their best, Hong Kong Moms' posts and membership have become notorious for out-of-touch close-mindedness, judgement, or just senselessness. The comments on these controversial posts are as riveting as the posts themselves with members jumping to criticise, jumping to defend, and jumping to criticise the defence and defend the critics. The average group member is a well-educated wife (note the Harvard diploma above the crib), with 2.5 children, a domestic helper, a nice Island-side apartment, a cute dog, and disposable income courtesy of her husband's investment banking job. Am I being reductive? Yes, but I will say that when I showed this to one of my aunties, she cackled, and said that if I changed the French bulldog to an Alsatian and the Harvard diploma to a Georgetown one, it would be her. The poem is made up of some of the more scandalous (or really just everyday) posts that I've seen on the group over the past two years. There's always a debate about the difference between a regular bed and a "helper bed" (beds in helpers' quarters are usually too small to fit a standard twin). There was a fight about a plant milk petition once. There was another kerfuffle about a woman's treatment of some saltwater fish that she could not keep alive in freshwater... It's a great source of entertainment. And also a great place to find an iHerb code.

SOPHIA HOTUNG

HONG KONG MOMS 心靜自然涼 • A woman peruses the Hong Kong Moms Facebook group while domestic chaos rages around her. Based on the December 7, 2020 New Yorker magazine cover *Love Life* by Adrian Tomine.

let's play the wheel stakes are high
for one hundred nothing too steep
now stop that wheel
what have we got
your kid's been born a sheep

for five hundred give me a letter
we're looking for a sign
now stop that wheel
what have we got
your kid's come out as swine

now final round let's spin that wheel
ten thousand you wanna switch
now stop that wheel
what have we got
your kid's come out a bitch

Horoscope Zoetrope replaces the astrological signs in the original New Yorker cover with zodiac signs, and Mother Goose nursery lore with products or brands linked to Hong Kong. Starting on the far left, you have McDull representing the pig, Hong Kong Phooey representing the dog, glazed restaurant window chickens representing the rooster, the Monkey King representing the monkey, the sheep from a series of banned political books representing the ram, the Hong Kong Jockey Club logo representing the horse, snake oil medicine representing the serpent, the bygone Dragonair airline logo representing the dragon, White Rabbit candies representing the rabbit, Tiger Balm patches representing the tiger, (my favourite vending machine drink) Vitasoy chocolate milk representing the ox, and finally Hong Kong Disneyland's Mickey Mouse representing the rat. The poem borrows language from "spin the wheel" game shows and references the arbitrariness of how some parents believe that their children's personalities and prospects are defined by the year or month during which they burst out of their mother.

SOPHIA HOTUNG

HOROSCOPE ZOETROPE 日蝕月食 • The zodiac animals, represented on a wheel by capitalist, colonial, traditional, political, and cultural Hong Kong symbols. Based on the September 30, 1991 New Yorker magazine cover *Mother Goose Zodiac* by J.B. Handelsman.

THE HONG KONGER ANTHOLOGY

        much have i backpacked in asia on gap years
        and many malls and euro alcoves seen
        round many thai islands have i been
        about which trivago and travel bloggers rave
        but of one home comfort i've been told
        about which even karens don't find complaint
        its wide range of shortbread its trove of cheese bags
        a middle-aged blonde yelling at a local cashier
        i felt like a man back home on the high street
        picking up prawn cocktail elderflower brie
like a kid browsing percy pigs and jammy dodger packets
        unaware he could stare out at the china sea
        and behind fan the figures foreign to these joys
        strangers to squash and potted eton mess
        while i look from aisle to aisle with a wild surmise
        silently gorging back up to the peak up from m&s

View of the World from M&S continues my crusade to mock expats, even though I also do a lot of expat things like shop at Marks & Spencer for their gluten-free Colombian coffee and walnut cake. The New Yorker equivalent of this print, Saul Steinberg's *View of the World from 9th Avenue*, actually was the first Hong Konger I ever tried to make. I never finished the first version of it, but I did feel like the concept would strike a chord within the expatriate community, so I made another Hong Konger, *Room with a View*, posted it to Instagram, got a positive response, and thus began this whole palaver. The print's joke is based on expats' general reluctance to leave the more anglicised island and do battle with Chinese characters and Cantonese slang across the Harbour in Kowloon and the New Territories. You'll often see in the Hong Kong Moms Facebook group requests for help finding a Halloween costume or an iPhone screen repair shop specifically near Central, the home turf. I adapted John Keats's *On First Looking into Chapman's Homer*, because it's about exploring new frontiers and therefore contrasts greatly with the confinement of English-speaking Hong Kongers to English-speaking alcoves of the city. Keats's poem's most famous line is its last, "Silent upon a peak in Darien", and I could not resist the pun on peak, linking it to the most historic of expat neighbourhoods, the Peak.

SOPHIA HOTUNG

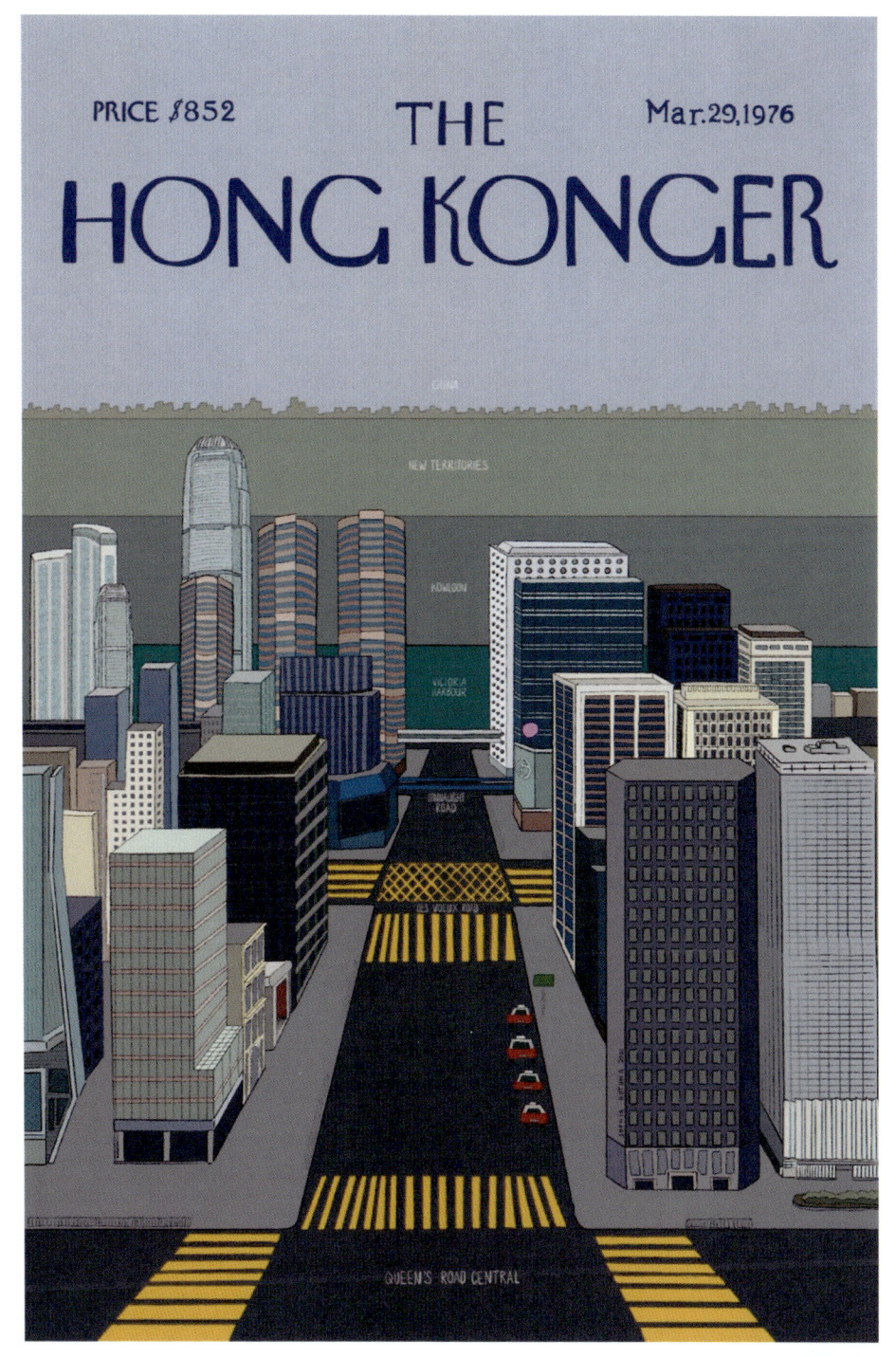

VIEW OF THE WORLD FROM M&S 城市追擊 • A view of the world from a Hong Kong Islander expatriate's perspective. Based on the March 29, 1976 New Yorker magazine cover *View of the World from 9th Avenue* by Saul Steinberg.

THE HONG KONGER ANTHOLOGY

the gweilos came down from their mid-levels home
with their children's eyes glued to ipad and iphone
and the sheen of their porsche was like sweat on their skin
as they balked at the smells and winced at the din

for the kwun tong bypass spread her arms down the bay
and spat dust on the shield of their convertiblé
and the eyes of the parents roamed nervous and scared
once they passed the tollbooths and paid the steep fare

but there lay the dark side distorted and grey
with road signs in green and canto in play
legend has it they roamed 'til the day was gone
then were lost forever to the back and beyond

Dark Side depicts the expats who *do* make it through the Cross-Harbour Tunnel to Kowloon, unlike those that choose to stay within spitting distance of Marks & Spencer (flip back a page to understand the reference). The New Yorker equivalent shows a family driving along Route 95 from Connecticut to Manhattan. Long Island Sound, the body of water between Long Island and Connecticut, is now Victoria Harbour and Route 95 is now the Kwun Tong Bypass. The family drives an expensive red Porsche and the two older children are decked out in designer headphones and quintessential Gen Z fashion. I even gave the mother a spiky, chunky-highlighted, Karen-esque haircut, because I was feeling deeply scathing. The poem is an adaptation of the *Destruction of Sennacherib* by Lord Byron, which is a rhythmic poem about the Assyrian siege of Jerusalem in the Bible. The poem sounds intrepid, which is what driving in unfamiliar parts of Hong Kong can feel like with impatient taxi drivers honking at you, nobody indicating before changing lanes, and lots of aggressive undertaking.

SOPHIA HOTUNG

DARK SIDE 人地生疏 • An expat family warily traverses the Kwun Tong Bypass, unfamiliar with their Kowloon-side surroundings. Based on the August 7, 1937 New Yorker magazine cover by William Steig.

a painted boat harbouring whiners
urgent rhythms and pressing tunes
heaves chipped reptilian wood
through water thick sand dunes

the clouds give traction 'neath the boat
and cling to the oars long enough
for the pulse to grow louder and drag to last longer
through glue waves sticky and tough

flurry of butterflies clamour of bees
all dance and buzz in ears
to be swatted away by blistered palms
drenched from sweat and tears

the clear day slows the lagging boat
men burst in the warmth bright red
oars in seaweed oars in debris
lifted out of the water each tread

this is not a sport for ghosts
who haunt these bays then leave
leave them to their shaded peaks
to languidly eat mulberries

Dragon Riders replaced a regatta rowing crew in its equivalent New Yorker cover with a dragon boat team. Dragon Boat Festival is a local holiday more familiar to expats, with many training for and competing in the races, which take place on the fifth day of the fifth lunar month, so normally in June. *Dragon Riders* depicts an international crew of rowers with a local drummer keeping the rhythm. The poem, adapted from Ouyang Xiu's *Deep in Spring, the Rain Has Passed (Picking Mulberries)*, comes from the perspective of a local who is protective of his culture from foreigners. He implies that gweilos have no place competing in Chinese traditions like dragon boat racing and that even nature is against the practice. For all my satirising of expat culture, I do find the conversation about what Hong Kong activities foreigners are and aren't allowed to participate in to be reduced to rules that often ignore mixed race or well-meaning individuals and encourage cultural segregation. I try to be sensitive to how I portray elements of Hong Kong without orientalising, exploiting, or fetishising it, but sometimes can still be called out as an appropriative gweimui. At the end of the day, I think all anyone can do is listen and make concerted efforts to learn.

SOPHIA HOTUNG

DRAGON RIDERS 龍之船人 • An exhausted dragon boat team burn out as their drummer urges them to press on. Based on the June 15, 1935 New Yorker magazine cover by Garrett Price.

101

THE HONG KONGER ANTHOLOGY

              this morning we had sun then rain
       so the ground was mulchy my feet got wet
            i packed a mud ball into my hands
       and rubbed the silken silt finger-tween
             we are not lost out in the sticks
            we are familiar and we are home
            but far off come the borachios
                 pickled and puking
               seasick and sensitive
               to the sun and the rain
           and our home beyond the clouds
            happy hearted we watch one
        stumble chunder fall in the sea

Yacht Yahoos pairs up with *Dragon Riders* in some ways, except this print highlights westerners in Hong Kong who come out for the high-flying lifestyle and do little to understand or educate themselves about local culture. In the print, four expats sail past stilt houses in Tai O Fishing Village, a tourist location to visitors but a neighbourhood to locals. It is implied that the sailors are drunk, loud, and ostentatious, and the poem, adapted from Yue Fu's *Sun and Rain*, contrasts these attributes with an unsuspecting villager who has just woken up and sees them approach.

SOPHIA HOTUNG

PRICE $852 **THE** **Aug. 7, 1954**
HONG KONGER

YACHT YAHOOS 落井下石 • A crew of expats sail past the stilt villages of Tai O Fishing Village on a lofty yacht. Based on the August 7, 1954 New Yorker magazine cover by Garrett Price.

oh she's a dear now isn't she lovely
well that's exotic isn't it marian
i told her i said you better come out here
it's just so warm like a day down in brighton
humidity quite heavy just look at my hair
but it is lovely isn't it oh it just is it is
oh this is lovely look at her jewellery
i just love all these oriental cultures
i tried a pho yesterday great to get some
authentic food while we're out here
i've recently discovered dai pai dongs
oh you have to come they're raucous fun
nige sat on one of those plastic stools
it crumbled beneath him oh i know
You'd think the asian diet would be
better for his cholesterol
oh i didn't notice her lovely hat
well that is lovely oh i wish i knew what it was called
not that i could pronounce it correctly
oh hello yes how do you say this
oh that's awfully complicated it really is just a hat
oh she's waking up she's waking up
she won't mind it's all so lovely out here

Pink Ladies replaces its New Yorker counterpart's Native American with the Empress Dowager Cixi. She was a fearsome matriarch of the Qing dynasty, and therefore a great contradiction to the western pre-conception that Asian women are soft, demure, and subservient. The joke of the print is that the two white (or pink) ladies have assumed that Cixi is another feeble Asian lady with "lovely", "oriental" jewellery, a lady whom they can infantalise and patronise with well-meaning but ignorant comments. The poem is from the perspective of one of these pink ladies, talking to a friend about her move to Hong Kong and experiences with local people and environments. It completes an unintentional Hong Konger triptych, which also includes *Dragon Riders* and *Yacht Yahoos*, about the consumption of Hong Kong culture by white foreigners, and tries to provide examples of appropriation and appreciation, encouraging readers to draw their own conclusions, rules, and exceptions to what's respectful or "allowed".

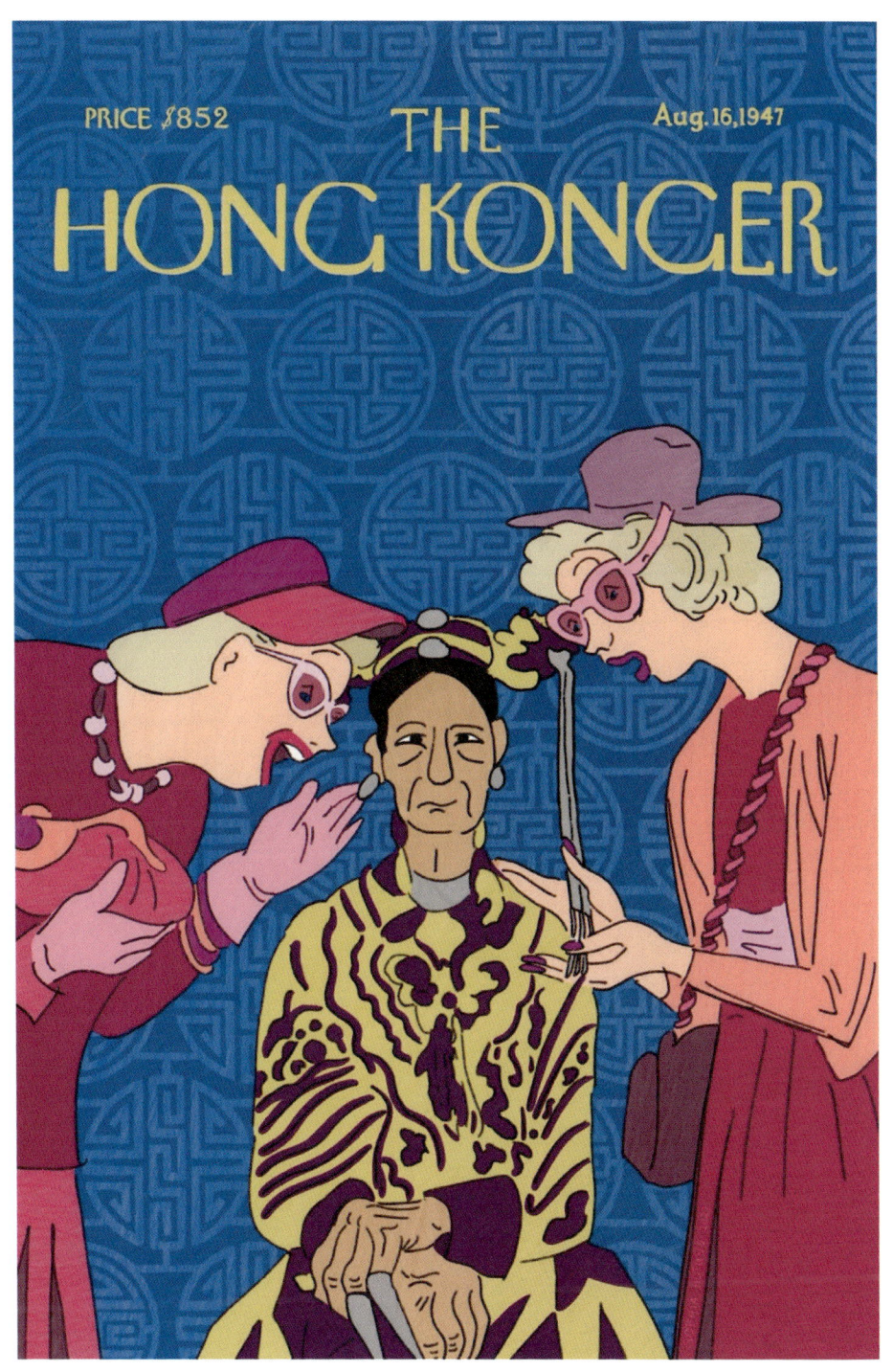

PINK LADIES 母儀天下 • Two blonde ladies coo and patronise the fearsome Empress Dowager Cixi. Based on the August 16, 1947 New Yorker magazine cover by Julian de Miskey.

105

THE HONG KONGER ANTHOLOGY

i'd like my money back
where the hell is king kong
the brochure said to expect
exoticism on all fronts
and we have yet to see
a panda doing kung fu
a batman heist
a one inch punch coolie battle
a tomb raider chase on fishing boats
an indiana jones doom temple
a casino triad kidnapping
a freaky friday body swap
i'll settle for a gong sound
or just my money back

Groundlings is often read as a comment on how screen-obsessed people have become, given that, in the print, spectators are watching a movie, totally unaware of a monster battle going on in Victoria Harbour. However, I actually set out to critique western movies' depiction of Hong Kong as an exotic, futuristic city. Hollywood seems to think Hong Kong is where mad scientists develop creatures in labs, dubious triads have kungfu fights on harbour pontoons, and lithe ladies in cheongsams and red lipstick seduce you at the craps table. Hollywood gives Hong Kong far too much credit for being sexy, swashbuckling, and intriguing. *Groundlings* therefore plays along with that narrative, almost as if to say, "Sure, we have King Kong and Godzilla here. It's no big deal. We just carry on with our days." The poem, meanwhile, reflects the viewpoint of a tourist who's come out to see the aforementioned sights, only to find a normal city with tired commuters, stressed students, and bad traffic. The name *Groundlings* is a pun and portmanteau that combines the name of the outdoor cinema, The Grounds, and the word "earthlings" or "underlings", which is what most ordinary people in movies like *Godzilla vs. Kong* are.

SOPHIA HOTUNG

PRICE $852   THE   AUG. 24, 2009

HONG KONGER

GROUNDLINGS 百年難得一見 • An outdoor screening of "Godzilla vs. Kong" at the Grounds in AIA Vitality Park distracts from a real battle between the beasts by Victoria Harbour. Based on the August 24, 2009 New Yorker magazine cover *Double Feature* by Adrian Tomine.

107

THE HONG KONGER ANTHOLOGY

      we need a way to cross old vic
        the car ferry runs too slow
to get to the club for a smoke and a nap
       there must be a fast way to go

      we need a way to cross old vic
       the tunnel runs too jammed
to get island side for a meeting and steak
      there must be an upper hand

      we need a way to cross old vic
       the autotoll runs too low
  so press the gas and jerk the wheel
   and over the tollbooth you'll go

Autotoll reminds me of the toy cars that I used to play with on the carpet we had with roads and highways stitched into it. Therefore, when I wrote the poem, I wanted a repetitive, childlike, nursery rhyme rhythm. I also find that cars in Hong Kong are a great visual representation of the wealth gap, since some Hong Kongers collect garages of swanky Teslas, hefty Rolls Royces, and zippy Minis, while other Hong Kongers make use of public transport. The language in the poem about "the club", "meeting and steak", and "smoke and a nap" reflect an old boys' club mentality common in driving clubs. I interviewed a car photographer and blogger, Adrian Ma, while working on *Autotoll* and its poem. Adrian discussed the cat-and-mouse game that car enthusiasts play with law enforcement when it comes to upgrades, as well as the culture around Sunday morning drives and vehicular clubs.

AUTOTOLL 飛車 • Hong Kong's most luxurious and popular cars soar over tunnel tollbooths. Based on the December 9, 2002 New Yorker magazine cover by Bruce McCall.

i met a restaurateur from a frantic land
who said one vast and submerged hull of stoves
sits in the water near it by the dock
half drunk a glutton trio bob cigars
ablaze and bellies full and sneer of foes' failures
brag that their menus full men's palettes feed
which yet endure burned on their serpent tongues
the hand that cooked them and the dish that fed
and on the dinner bill these words appear
behold the michelin series b funding gold-plated forks
look on our feasts ye foodies and gorge
nothing consumed remembered wiped around the plate
of a decadent rich meal buttonless and binging
the tourists and critics lumber off to bed

Closing Time turned a Titanic-themed New Yorker cover about the stock market into a comment on Hong Kong's competitive restaurant industry. There are a handful of large restaurant groups that umbrella multiple eateries in Hong Kong. Their established position enables them to out-compete smaller mom-and-pop spots and individual restaurants struggling to manage with high rents, picky diners, and Covid-19 restrictions. The print is therefore a comment on well-funded megaliths managing to stay afloat (literally), while less endowed establishments cave. I chose to illustrate the Jumbo Floating Restaurant not because I was under the impression that it was an underdog in the industry (it was not), but because it's a big boat (and I needed to replace the New Yorker's Titanic with a big boat) and the idea of it going down reminded me of the scene in the 1988 TV miniseries adaptation of James Clavell's *Noble House*. The poem adapts Percy Bysshe Shelley's *Ozymandias*, a poem about the futility of seeking immortal fame, which I thought was particularly relevant given the ephemerality of food that disappears down a gullet or expires soon after being prepared.

SOPHIA HOTUNG

CLOSING TIME 吃喝玩樂 • Pretentious chefs flee the scene of a burning Jumbo Floating Restaurant, one with a dubious lighter in hand. Based on the August 15 & 22, 2011 New Yorker magazine cover *S.O.S.* by Christoph Niemann.

a ground-breaking idea so we're asking for a bil
now hear us out i only want to take a minute
it's an invention beyond the scope of human fathoment
now i'll lift up the tarp but please promise not to scream
whoosh as you can see it's large it's complex
and only my team are equipped to work the gears
the funding we're after is only series b
now watch as it brews this cup of weak tea

Order Up is the only Hong Konger that is also an animated gif. Its animated alter-ego shows tea dripping into and splashing out of the teacup, much like the coffee in Christoph Niemann's also animated New Yorker equivalent does. Every gizmo and gadget in the print is a Chinese invention ranging from the standard sidafaming (the "four great inventions" of gunpowder, paper, printing, and the compass), to obviously Chinese items like the banjo-esque ruan and stringed guzheng, to more zany paraphernalia like the diablo and beckoning cat figurines. It's more of a celebration of China's history of engineering rather than Hong Kong's, and that's emphasised with the Qing dynasty man holding the teacup. The poem mocks and mimics my generation's up-and-coming wave of tech entrepreneurs who are flooding the Greater Bay Area, scooping up venture capitalist funding, and raring to build the next sexiest app, which usually isn't all that sexy or ground-breaking.

ORDER UP 萬大發明 • A Qing dynasty inventor brews a cup of tea using inventions from ancient Chinese history. Based on the November 16, 2015 New Yorker magazine cover *Coffee Break* by Christoph Niemann.

hey sorry i'm running late
there's commotion on nathan road
i'm stuck in traffic while we wait
for the cannons to reload
order me a daquiri
but decant some in a glass
as i've been hit a little bit
while trying to sidle past

Kowloon Motor Battalion was one of the last prints that I ideated and created. While there is no overwhelmingly famous bus rivalry in New York, when I saw two warring double-deckers, I immediately thought of the eponymous Kowloon Motor Bus and Island-side First Bus. KMB is the largest bus company in Hong Kong, with First Bus being the third. (Citybus, which is owned by the same parent company as First Bus, is the second.) Driving in Hong Kong can be a hazard with aggressive taxi drivers and swerving two-storey buses. On Nathan Road, a busy thoroughfare that cuts northward through a handful of bustling neighbourhoods like Tsim Sha Tsui, Mong Kok, and Yau Ma Tei, it's even more high-stakes. This print upped the ante even more by turning Nathan Road into a battleground. The poem marries the intense warlike scene with the mundanity of running late to meet a friend for drinks. My mother pointed out after I had already sold a few prints of *Kowloon Motor Battalion* that the buses are on the wrong side of the road. She had a point. The rebuttal I had to generate on the spot for being caught out was that much like with *Ghosts of Punters Past*, I'm depicting a backwards world where it would be understandable for buses to travel into oncoming traffic.

KOWLOON MOTOR BATTALION 不共戴天 • A Kowloon Motor Bus and a First Bus pass in the night, cannons flying from their gun ports. Based on the July 20, 2009 New Yorker cover *Tour Wars* by Bruce McCall.

what will make people call this art
i have seen at the tate papers bleached black
paint splashed and thought i could do that
i have seen people naked in exhibitions
blotches sold for mint in limited editions

me i have a brush and paint in a can
and i colourise walls as an aestetician
but i am no artist as no one comes to see
no one comes for photographs
no one comes for me

but put me in a white boxed room
play a mournful jazzy song
call it a performance piece
and in will pour the throng

Scaffolds & Spills has a backstory about my father, which only seems fair given how much I've yammered on about my mother and Popo by now. An eccentric man, for lack of a better word, my father once woke me up on a Sunday morning by balancing on scaffolding outside my bedroom window, painting our village house. For the print, I relocated my father and his bamboo to Graham Street against the backdrop of a well-known outdoor mural of village houses, painted by Alex Croft. The poem raises the question of defining a difference between art and painting. The painter who coloured the wall that Croft would eventually create a mural on would not be considered an artist for that particular paint-job, but Croft would for his mural. One could argue that it's because Croft drew an intricate scene while the painter just used blue. But that calls into question a lot of modern art. The poem comes from the perspective of the wall-painter and raises ideas about how context — usually supported by money and race — influence how we decide what is art and what is just painting a wall.

SOPHIA HOTUNG

SCAFFOLDS & SPILLS 千鈞一髮 • A painter loses his balance on bamboo scaffolding while touching up wall paint above local artist Alex Croft's mural on the corner of Graham Street and Hollywood Road. Based on the April 2, 2012 New Yorker magazine cover *Rite of Spring* by George Booth.

117

THE HONG KONGER ANTHOLOGY

i do not know what i sing i've only learned the sounds
i've memorised the telling-offs when i mis-move my mouth
i've memorised when to react and when it's right to sing
i've memorised the feeling of my throat curdling a ring
i came down here to hear my name to feel a limelight burn
model singer dancer swinger nothing took its turn
but there are nights i sing to no-one in our empty hall
and since i don't know what I sing am i singing at all

Opera Girl was one of the last poems I wrote for the book. I was contemplating what constitutes art after writing the poem for *Scaffolds & Spills* and wondered how much of art relied on its consumption and reception. *Opera Girl* shows a woman who has migrated from Mainland China to become a Cantonese opera singer, which you can tell from the Chinese opera placards above her mirror. However, in the poem, the reader learns that she does not actually understand Cantonese and has only memorised sounds. I set up the narrative to convey imposter syndrome, a sense of disconnect, and self-doubt. I then brought in this idea of "if a tree falls but no one hears it, does it make a sound?" That philosophical question was posed as early as 1883 in the magazine *The Chautauquan* and was answered with the explanation that because "sound is the sensation excited in the ear when the air or other medium is set in motion," that no, the tree's crash to the ground would not make a sound. Given that I had always created art and just never showed people for much of my life until now, it made me wonder if it still counted as art. Superficially, the answer should be: "Yes! If you call it art, it's art!" but I think every artist has their doubts about whether their work is only meaningful when it is received well by others.

OPERA GIRL 胭脂水粉 • A Chinese opera singer prepares her make-up backstage at the Sunbeam Theatre. Based on the April 3, 1948 New Yorker magazine cover by Constantin Alajalov.

when they put degas in the met
and calder in the gug
who did they plan for them to greet
not a moustache and a birkin and a disposable camera
that flashed and was chided for bleaching the paints

when they named the cloisters
for its connecting points
or the whitney for a woman with cash and clay
who did they plot for them to welcome
not pram-idle babes and air-con hounds
that take up benches wiping gum on velvet

when they labelled specific places
landmarks city plaza elements alike
who did they plot for them to enthral
but tourists tycoons tai tais
with platinum heeled shoes and fur lined watches
zen-scented ascots and snake-oiled veneers
rouge-caked eyelids and charcoal-veined cheque-books
who sip champagne in the changing room and touch all the art

Mallseum, a pun on "mall" and "museum", replaces artworks in the Guggenheim Museum with shop windows in a generic glassy Hong Kong shopping mall. Museum culture, though strong in New York, is weak here. We have history, space, science, and other museums but they are hardly places that average Hong Kongers visit outside of a school field trip. On a rainy day, Hong Kongers go to malls, not museums. The poem is loosely inspired by Ada Limón's *A Name*, which was my favourite poem that the Poetry Society of America posted as part of their Poetry in Motion campaign on the 1 train in New York while I was at college. The poem begins, "When Eve walked among / the animals and named them", and the first lines of my first stanzas mimic that structure.

MALLSEUM 行街街 • Window shoppers peer at displays in a luxury shopping mall. Based on the March 17, 1975 New Yorker magazine cover by Laura Jean Allen.

THE HONG KONGER ANTHOLOGY

let us go then you and i
while the harbour still drifts out against the sky
like a corpse formaldehyded on a table
let us go down from spectator-speckled piers
the muttering redactions of middle-agers
nibbling nails nervously as the wizened take the plunge
strokes that follow like the gentle talks
that connect the mornings to lunch
and lunches to eves
propel us north and out to meet
the schooners and ferries
her majesty's ships
the cargo the tugboat
let us go and make our visit
for we have grown old we have grown old
on a faerie land we shall walk upon the shore
hear the mermaids singing over the score
of mourners dying the white hair of the waves
while we danced in the chambers of the sea
white hair white skin we drown

Splash Harbour was one of the first four Hong Kongers that I ideated but was the penultimate Hong Konger that I finished. In fact, I re-started it from scratch a week before sending this book to print, because I felt that my technique had improved since the beginning and the concept deserved better. The print is a celebration of elderly Hong Kongers' spry and active approach to exercise in old age. My Popo was trekking, walking, and riding rollercoasters well into her 70s until she passed away at 78, and she was no exception to many athletic, older Hong Kongers who swim, practise taichi, and hike. The print is a celebration, but the poem is more morbid. I adapted T.S. Eliot's *The Love Song of J. Alfred Prufrock*, which I found deeply confounding in college and still find to this day. I like *Prufrock* for its spectral images and breathless rhythm. Therefore, given my interpretation, I created a scene of old people welcoming death and travelling to their next lives by diving into the Harbour and swimming across to the after-life, almost as if the Harbour were the River Styx. It's not a sad or dark depiction of death. It's one of acceptance, assurance, and adventure, which are the feelings I believe my Popo had when she died.

SOPHIA HOTUNG

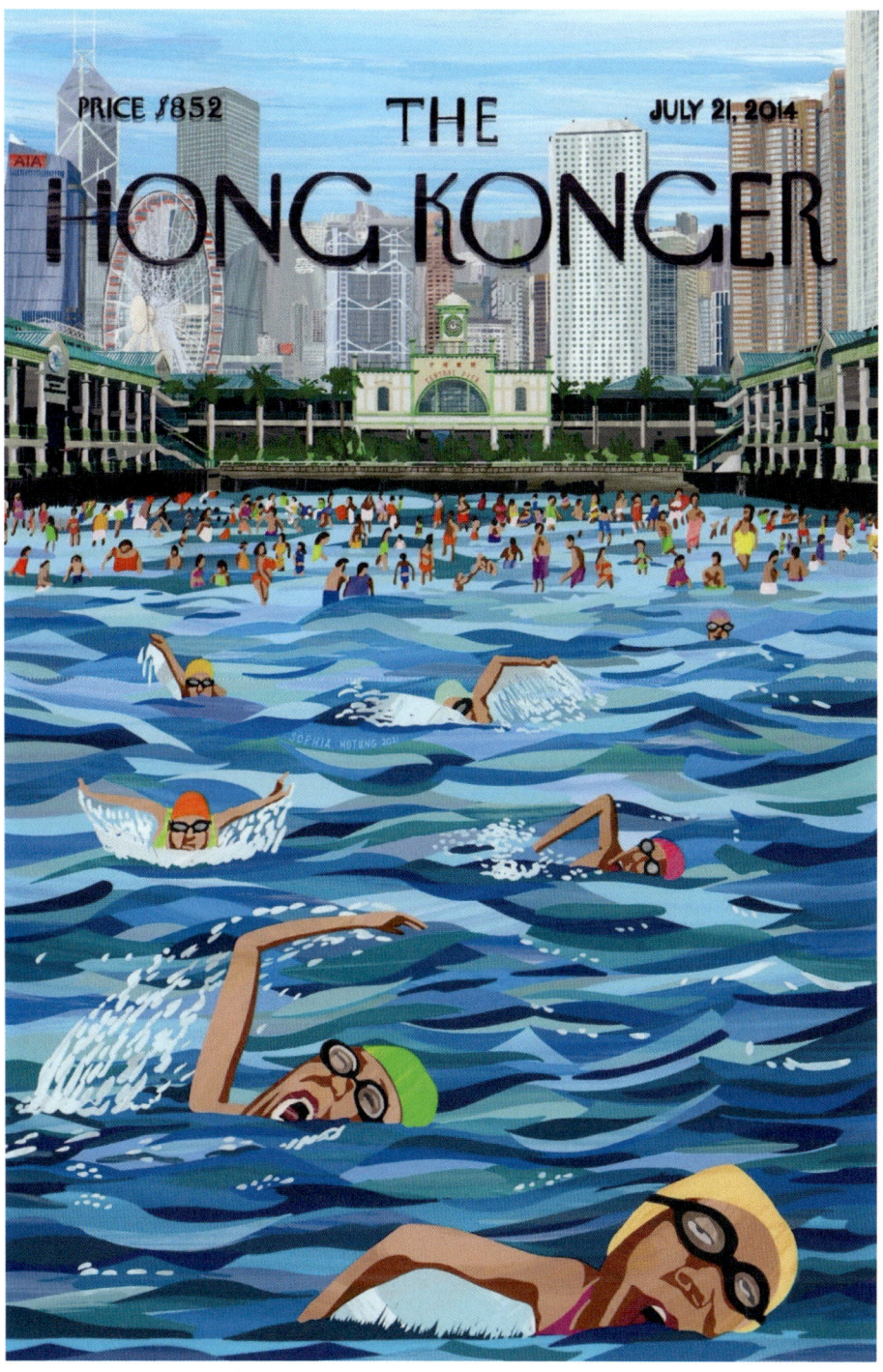

SPLASH HARBOUR 老襯盪北 • Swimmers practise their front crawl in Victoria Harbour by Central Piers on a hot summer day. Based on the July 21, 2014 New Yorker magazine cover *Coney Island* by Mark Ulriksen.

THE HONG KONGER ANTHOLOGY

the pomelo leaf the fresh pyjama silk
the ivory comb the gatecrashing fee
the jujubes and lotus seeds
the tea and the porcelain it came in

the mahjong sets and linen tablecloths
the mistress who picked the date
the drinking train first-class berths
the av man a lascivious uncle

the dried shrimp in vacuum seals
fruits from japan in baskets
hessian sacks of rice and beans
red and greens distracting hens

bridal cakes and crisp dollar bills
tucked into the fold of the hamper
gold and red and tinsel
my mother thinks is tacky

we fold up the umbrella
and climb in a cab
$24 what we have left
to take us 2km away

Just Cabbied is another one of my earliest prints which replaces traditional western wedding clothes and a yellow cab with traditional Chinese wedding clothes and a red cab. Since I created this Hong Konger so early on in the project, it's a more literal translation of New York to Hong Kong and lacks the personal stories that I started building into subsequent prints. The poem goes through the extravagant elements of a Hong Kong wedding from gifts to food to rituals, set against the backdrop of a mundane taxi ride, a cheap fare, and even an obscure uncle working the photo slideshow at the banquet.

SOPHIA HOTUNG

JUST CABBIED 車鈎 • A newly married couple speeds off in a Hong Kong red taxi. Based on the June 25, 2007 New Yorker magazine cover by Lou Romano.

THE HONG KONGER ANTHOLOGY

the guest list was short
on the glassine card paper
we sent invites on

but we weren't alone
i heard them sing in the pews
i heard rice hit the flagstone

they were with us there
weeping phantom celebrants
watching their daughter's

daughter's daughter wed
the men of the ancestry
floating up from the

celtic cross where we
reflect on how they were killed
not rolling in graves

over how with us
your fathers and my fathers
no longer battle

this hall was our church
this hall was your wartime club
stripped stained glass windows

raped desecrated
but we do not think on this
as we leave the doors

and step out into
the shade of a banyan tree
all seeing all love

St John's Cathedral is my anglicised take on Hong Kong weddings. St John's is the oldest Anglican church in East Asia and was declared a Hong Kong monument in 1996. During World War II and Japan's occupation of Hong Kong, the Cathedral served as a clubhouse for the Japanese military, who brutalised not only my father's Hong Kong family but also my Popo's Shanghainese family. My mother was forbidden from stepping foot in Japanese department stores as a girl and first tasted sushi on her first date with my father. When I started dating my partner Spencer, who is half Japanese, she joked that our ancestors would be turning in their graves. The poem is a meditation on a hypothetical wedding between Spencer and me in St John's Cathedral (which, for the record, would be unlikely given that he is Jewish and I'm a lapsed Catholic). The poem describes the Hong Konger bride's ghostly ancestors watching the union and acknowledges the horrors of the Japanese occupation while offering a restorative dénouement rooted in love.

ST JOHN'S CATHEDRAL 白頭偕老 • Newly-weds leave St John's Cathedral on Garden Road. Based on the June 2, 1934 New Yorker magazine cover by Harry Brown.

bright star my sin was too much hope of thee
though skies across the way show not this gloom
love lies not with this crude rule and decree
but feeds itself to sand the edge of doom
so long as men may breathe and eyes may see
so long as plumes may scrawl and script may dry
so long the fears that love may cease to be
then long the street will sound its battle cry
o for my sake do not with fortune chide
nor in lone splendour curse the night bright star
since brass nor stone nor earth nor boundless tide
shall halt the minds that now converted are
lo in the orient that gracious light
lifts up his burning head to colour night

Courtship, a print about love, needed as much reinforcement from as many love poems as possible. I adopted the Renaissance sonnet form, and any keen-eyed bibliophiles will notice that I've lifted lines and phrases from Shakespeare's Sonnets 7, 65, 111, and 116; Ben Jonson's sonnet *On My First Son*, and John Keats's *Bright Star, Would I Were Stedfast as Thou Art*. The print and poem reflect the ongoing efforts to achieve marriage equality in Hong Kong. Astute viewers will notice the faint rainbow along the road, shining between a crack in the barricades. It functions as a symbol of hope and tenacity.

SOPHIA HOTUNG

PRICE $852   THE   MAY 21, 2012
HONG KONGER

COURTSHIP 明天會更好 • Hong Kong's Old Supreme Court Building hints at a future of marriage equality. Based on the May 21, 2012 New Yorker magazine cover *Spectrum of Light* by Bob Staake.

THE HONG KONGER ANTHOLOGY

>our love was planned as a run of pure pongs
>a triplet for the table to behold
>my heart my soul my mind sweetly aligned
>a game to play to sikwu not to fold
>but your runs hold tong zi next to green sok
>and winds blow south though you're the banking east
>you hide your hand from view but i can count
>you hold fourteen there at the very least
>shall i disrupt the game and tear the walls
>reveal the undersides of cards falling
>or should i wait for what's to never come
>you hold the block to win that i'm calling
>oh who's to win when it's not left to luck
>but left to those who play chicken and duck

Valentine's Cards was created at a time where I thought I'd make a calendar or greeting cards of seasonal Hong Kongers. I changed New Yorker playing cards to Hong Konger mahjong cards as a tribute to my Popo, who taught all five of her white-washed grandchildren to play. For the poem, I used the sonnet form, much like I did with *Courtship*, as it's a stereotypical form for love poems and has a satisfying, uniform structure, much like a winning mahjong hand. The content is bleak, however, touching upon a relationship tainted by infidelity and adultery. The final reference to "chicken and duck" is a term that Sean, the project's translator, and I discussed at length, because I was convinced that it's a slang term used in mahjong, but after doing research, we're pretty sure my Popo reworded the actual term: 雞胡 or "chicken hand". Outside of mahjong, "chicken and duck" refers respectively to "prostitutes and gigolos". In a mahjong context, according to Popo, "chicken and duck" is a winning hand in mahjong that mixes pongs (a triplet of the same card) and soengs (a triplet of three consecutive cards). She banned us from playing chicken and duck hands because they are easy to build, earn no points, and cut the game short, which can be frustrating when other players are taking their time to build complex, high-scoring hands. In the poem, there is a parallel between the chicken and duck cutting short a game with shoddy hands and infidelity cutting short a relationship.

SOPHIA HOTUNG

VALENTINE'S CARDS 愛情遊戲 • Mahjong cards, transformed for Valentine's Day. Based on the February 12, 2001 New Yorker magazine cover by Richard McGuire.

THE HONG KONGER ANTHOLOGY

> chick chick chick
> you hunch your neck and cluck
> your oily quills twitch under the whipping whirring fan
> your claws clench slowly as the cards are rearranged
>
> duck duck duck
> you flutter your wings sideways
> sets of triplets runs of siblings an easy win to steal
> a few fan here a few fan there what's another round

Chicken & Duck pairs well with *Valentine's Cards*, because now we get to see a real live chicken and duck game in full swing. The poem is based on the Tang Dynasty poem *Ode to the Goose* by Luo Binwang. An English translation of the poem begins: "Goose, goose, goose, / You bend your neck towards the sky and sing. / Your white feathers float on the emerald water, / Your red feet push the clear waves." In this parody, "goose" has been replaced by "chick" and "duck". As mentioned with *Valentine's Cards*, chicken and duck hands in mahjong are considered "lazy" hands that mix different suits and garner no "fan" or money when they win. The depiction of the chicken and duck in the poem and print show two hustlers looking to make a quick buck through lazy chicken and duck hands to avoid paying out larger sums to more advanced and ambitious players.

SOPHIA HOTUNG

PRICE $852   **THE**   June 24, 1974

HONG KONGER

CHICKEN & DUCK 雞同鴨講 • A chicken and duck play "chicken and duck" hands of mahjong. Based on the June 24, 1974 New Yorker magazine cover by Andre Francois.

that's my last tai tai painted on the wall
looking as if she weren't at all
in dance clubs in wan chai on tuesday nights
exploring the ripples of fleshy boy sprites
do you fancy a go she was a bankable lass
myself now i'm happy to give her a pass
i sit in my quarters she sits in hers
separation enforced by the virus
she once had a heart made much too wild
in a tst loo we conceived our first child
the photographer chanced ma'am hold back that cough
it's blurring the image and you look quite off
that's when i heard that dissonant note
and spied the half-flush dead on her throat
soon after the clubs had shut us outside
from town club bar to beach club tides
the lads got together and compared our gals
we penned their obits and felt silken palls
not one man infected not one man caressed
our tai tais in bed with coronavirus

Tai Tai's Toy Boys was inspired by the Starlight Dance Club Covid-19 super-spreader scandal of November 2020 which the South China Morning Post called "the defining image of Hong Kong's fourth wave of coronavirus infections". 732 cases of coronavirus were logged after a 75-year-old patron of the dance club contracted Covid. It came out that affluent, older tai tais jived and bopped with young, male dance instructors at the club, sometimes spending the night with them or at least laying on a naughty smooch. The poem is based on Robert Browning's *My Last Duchess*, and stems from the perspective of one of the husbands. It's not subtle when you know the above context, so maybe the less said on *Tai Tai's Toy Boys* the better.

SOPHIA HOTUNG

TAI TAI'S TOY BOYS 太太吃鴨 • An affluent tai tai indulges in a sliver of cake as her topless butlers stand by. Based on the November 19, 1927 New Yorker magazine cover by Rea Irvin.

135

THE HONG KONGER ANTHOLOGY

please stand back from the closing doors
keep trotters to your side
offer your seat to a sheep in need
dragons please don't fly

keep pups on leads so they don't run off
and snakes from stealing refrain
rabbits keep six feet apart
we can't have any more on this train

rats please ride inside the cars
don't risk it on the tracks
horses careful with your shoes
don't lose them through the cracks

roosters keep from crowing
we have clocks overhead
and monkeys hang from handrails
if you find it hard to spread

oxen mind your ivory
it scrapes the ceiling paint
and tigers please don't eat riders
we can't get another complaint

New Year Transit, and the upcoming holiday Hong Kongers in this book, were fun pieces I created when I thought that I would turn the Hong Konger collection into a series of holiday cards or even a calendar. The animals are all zodiac animals riding the MTR, and the poem borrows language from MTR train announcements.

SOPHIA HOTUNG

NEW YEAR TRANSIT 飛黃騰達 • The zodiac animals ride a crowded MTR train. Based on the January 31, 1994 New Yorker magazine cover by Edward Sorel.

will you swim a little faster said the old rat to the ox
there's a tiger close behind us and he's treading on your socks
see how eagerly the dragon and the rabbit both advance
she is cruising on a logroll catching wind to join the dance
will you won't you will you won't you will you join the dance
will you won't you will you won't you won't you join the dance

you can really have no notion how delightful it will be
when the snake coils round and sends the horse straight out to sea
see the sheep bleat too far too far and give a look askance
the ape and cock help build a raft to ride and join the dance
will you won't you will you won't you will you join the dance
will you won't you will you won't you won't you join the dance

what matters is how far we go the dog to pig replies
there is another shore you know upon the other side
i'll stop to play you'll stop to feed no shame in dalliance
at least we shan't be slumbering like cat missing the dance
will you won't you will you won't you will you join the dance
will you won't you will you won't you won't you join the dance

Zodiac Divers lays out the zodiac animals in the order they cycle, starting with the rat and ending with the pig. They float right to left since Chinese is traditionally read in that direction, and they are in the sea as a reference to the swimming race legend that established the animals' order. When I started creating the print, I was going to draw the actual animals like with *New Year Transit*, but scale became an issue with the mouse and dragon ending up too small and too large respectively to appear consistent in the line-up. I liked the image of children wearing animal masks in the movie adaption of Stephen King's novel *Pet Sematary*, so I decided to mask the children in a similar way. The poem is based on *The Mock Turtle's Song* from Lewis Carroll's *Alice in Wonderland* sequel, *Through the Looking-Glass*. I always forget the order of the zodiac animals, so the poem names the animals in order — if you memorise the poem, you end up memorising the line-up too.

SOPHIA HOTUNG

PRICE $852   **THE**   **JULY 26, 2004**
THE HONG KONGER

ZODIAC DIVERS 十二仙過海 • Children, masked as the Chinese zodiac animals, ride a wave in the South China Sea. Based on the July 26, 2004 New Yorker magazine cover *Waves* by Jean-Jacques Sempé.

THE HONG KONGER ANTHOLOGY

we all know the man who lives in the moon
but this fellow dwells down here
he's round and soft with a heart of yolk
and in autumn loves to appear

he sets up his balcony out in mong kok
where the buildings are stacked nice and tight
and waits for the moon to shine on his wares
and glow in the cold amber night

his lanterns they gleam a fish and a moon
chang'e would be proud of the haven
he lives just as one like the moon sans the sun
the madcap mooncake maven

Mooncake Maven continues the streak of holiday-themed Hong Kongers with zany poems. The Chinese translation is literally 月餅人 or *Mooncake Man*, implying that the Maven is a man who not only loves mooncakes but also is made of mooncakes. There is no real agenda with this poem; I just wanted to celebrate the oddballs among us who are unabashedly enthusiastic about niche phenomena.

SOPHIA HOTUNG

PRICE $852   THE   DEC. 23, 2019
HONG KONGER

MOONCAKE MAVEN 月餅人 • A giddy hermit decks his balcony out for Mid-Autumn Festival. Based on the December 23, 2019 New Yorker magazine cover *Decking the Deck* by Edward Steed.

THE HONG KONGER ANTHOLOGY

the world is split into time zones
to help santa hurry along
if every town struck 12 at once
he'd burn out post-drop in hong kong

but by scaling the lines of longitude
and slaloming north then south
he's able to hit each chimneyed home
on time without burning out

hong kong well i've a question
how does he even get in
when chimneys are few to non-existent
and there are beep codes and prowling doormen

ah young child come sit on my lap
and i'll tell you a secret of his
you ever seen santa creep into your home
why no and the reason is this

when in lands like ours that are so padlocked tight
that the windows barely can shift
an army of elves are forced to sneak in
through the aircons and shafts in the lifts

reindeer are too dumb and santa too fat
to make it into the house
so they wait round the bend at an old cha chaan teng
eating dantat and fresh bolobaos

Santa at the Cha Chaan Teng started as an exercise in translating New York diner food into Hong Kong diner food. You can see that the coffee in the print has been replaced with dandanmian, bolobao, milk tea, and dantats, and even the elven barista's coffee machine has been swapped in for a wok and electric water heater. I wanted to create a few child-friendly holiday poems in a similar vein to *Zodiac Divers*, so based the corresponding poem on a theory I formulated as a kid about how time difference exists to facilitate Santa's global deliveries.

SOPHIA HOTUNG

SANTA AT THE CHA CHAAN TENG 為食老人 • Santa indulges in a Hong Kong-style café meal midway through delivering presents. Based on the December 17, 2018 New Yorker magazine cover *Santa's Little Helpers* by John Cuneo.

THE HONG KONGER ANTHOLOGY

        we tried to find the star
  not the tale of it but the glint itself
but my boswellian loot grows in mountains
        dry and high off the seas

   we reek of resin and seasickness
myrrh filling feebly the cracks in our boards
    the tarpaulin flapping hole-ridden
    its gold link chinking and faint

  blessed adventurers will have masks
   flippers a book a camera a knife
our gifts that no one wants are rusted
        salted brined

     there is no ladder
but we are here to find a young thing
    to mould it and make it
    an offshoot of opium
   a stench an oil a coin

Junk of the Magi trades in a Nordic vessel for a junk boat and places the Three Wise Men in Victoria Harbour, with a silhouette of muggy Wan Chai in the background. The poem draws on Adrienne Rich's *Diving into the Wreck*, which also inspired *10,000 Faeries*. The poem comes from the point of view of the Three Kings who brought gifts to the baby Jesus. Here, I've imagined that they have ventured as Christian missionaries to Hong Kong. However, they have found that their gifts — gold, frankincense, and myrrh — have not been too helpful on their maritime voyage, and now they feel displaced and out-of-their-depth on foreign soil. It's a meditation on colonialism and western influence.

SOPHIA HOTUNG

PRICE $852   **THE**   **Dec. 21, 1968**

THE HONG KONGER

JUNK OF THE MAGI 仙舨游 • The three wise men sail a junk boat down Victoria Harbour. Based on the December 21, 1968 New Yorker magazine cover by Charles Martin.

THE HONG KONGER ANTHOLOGY

two door signs one lies
it makes no difference to you
you can't read chinese

Portals is a big fan favourite, but it carries absolutely no symbolic meaning. A lot of people try to read the doors' signs or think that there is significance with the six colours, but I actually just wanted to troll viewers by writing Chinese that has no insidious message and illustrating doors in pretty colours that have no agenda. The poem is a haiku that draws on the famous riddle about two doors with two guards, one of whom always lies, one of whom always tells the truth. How does one know which guard to believe? The haiku points out that the whole riddle doesn't even matter if you can't understand either guard. Before the poem took the form of a haiku, it read as a more pointed jab at international school students like myself, who grow up in Hong Kong their whole lives but never learn Cantonese fluently because speaking it is often banned in schools. That poem went: "two doors two signs / only one tells the truth / but you can't read either / you went to international school".

SOPHIA HOTUNG

PRICE $852 — THE — July 16, 1979
HONG KONGER

PORTALS 去年今日此門中 • Traditional, historical, and commonplace Hong Kong doors from across various districts and neighbourhoods. Based on the July 16, 1979 New Yorker magazine cover by Laura Jean Allen.

147

ABOUT THE AUTHOR

Sophia Hotung is a disabled, Eurasian writer and illustrator from Hong Kong.

She started her art career in March 2021 after receiving an iPad the previous Christmas. She now uses that iPad to create Hong Kongers on the app Procreate, and to hijack her unsuspecting neighbours' Bluetooth speakers.

Before becoming an iPad-wielding recluse, Sophia studied English, Economics, and History at Barnard College in New York with lofty dreams of becoming a corporate dogsbody at a consulting firm. When she wasn't attending networking events at the Harlem Dinosaur Bar-B-Que, she starred as the token British accent in Control Top, an all-female improv comedy group, and edited articles on a mouldy sofa in the *Columbia Daily Spectator* offices above a Pinkberry.

As a graduate, Sophia dabbled in IT audit, crisis communications, and business development. However, after cycling in and out of hospitals and hot desks for two years, she left the rat race at 26 to be a full-time sick person.

Through her writing and art, Sophia advocates for chronic illness patients and workers, as well as subverts and rethinks the ways we talk about disability, gender, race, and socio-economic disparities in Hong Kong and abroad.

ACKNOWLEDGEMENTS

This book would not have been possible without the following people.

JOANNA HOTUNG — The biggest privilege in the world is being your kid. I thought a lot about wording your acknowledgement, because one little paragraph in the part of the book that no one reads is a big kick in the goolies for someone like you. Thank you for starting Kids' Gallery and letting me grow up with art classes everyday. Thank you for putting the tiny child desks by your big one in your office so we could watch you work. Thank you for inspiring me to make a living out of hobbies. Thank you for never giving up on finding treatments and solutions for my health. Thank you for sending me to expensive schools then not getting mad when I majored in English. Thank you for letting me make my own decisions even when you've disagreed. Thank you for never shaming me when steroids made me ugly or illness made me sad. Thank you for our weird, accidental, Covid roommateship — one day they will make it a Netflix series, and we'll finally have something else to watch instead of scrolling aimlessly. I love you, Jojo!

SPENCER SHUBERT — Thank you for being my friend and business associate. Thank you for loving me when I cannot do things as much as when I can.

NICK AND NORA DE GUZMAN — I could not have done any of this without your care, support, and love. I have only been able to create my art and write this book because you have taken care of me, fed me, transported me, and looked out for me when I could not do it myself.

PROFESSOR HENRY L.Y. CHAN — We've come a long way, Dr Chan. Six diagnoses, two infusions, and too many appointments later, you have saved my life (on multiple occasions), believed me when it would have been easier to write off my fatigue and pain, and kept me going too many times to count. Thank you for never giving up on me.

BELLA NIGHTINGALE —You were the first person to teach me about feminism; you showed me Heaney and Keats, Carol Ann Duffy and E.M. Forster; you empowered me to dress up as a turnip snedder, pen conspiracy essays about *District and Circle*, and stage ridiculous plays. Thank you for rooting for me, encouraging me, and influencing so much of what I make and do now. I'm sure you've detected your and Mr Nightingale's impact in these poems.

JANICE AND SEAN NGIAM — It's the indomitable brother-sister duo! Janice, thank you for providing levity to the project through our hot chocolate-fuelled brainstorming, research, and venting sessions. Sean, thank you for not only translating but also interpreting all the titles and descriptions. I don't even know how to begin to rave about the wit, intellect, and creativity that went into all of them.

FRAN AYALA, ADRIAN MA, AND THE ANONYMOUS INTERVIEWEES — Your interviews put into perspective what *The Hong Konger Anthology* and the project's upcoming books could be. I am so grateful to you taking part in our often difficult conversations about your experiences and lives in Hong Kong.

Printed in Great Britain
by Amazon